The namesake of this book comes from the 1980 Comedy film “The Gods Must Be Crazy,” in which an empty Coca-Cola bottle is dropped from a plane onto a community of African bushmen. The bottle is a gift from the gods, but after it leads to in-fighting among the villagers, the tribal leaders decide to return it to the gods by having one of the village elder journeys to the end of the world to drop the bottle over the edge. Through my own metaphorical coke bottle, I can see the dawn of a new empire. This book serves as a testament to my views on restoring the current empire (capitalism and enterprises) before it is too late.

PRAYER TO BRING BACK THE HOUSE OF ROOSEVELTS

"And they came to Jerusalem. And he entered the temple and began to drive out those who sold and those who bought in the temple, and he overturned the tables of the money-changers and the seats of those who sold pigeons. And he would not allow anyone to carry anything through the temple. And he was teaching them and saying to them, "Is it not written, 'My house shall be called a house of prayer for all the nations'? But you have made it a den of robbers." And the chief priests and the scribes heard it and were seeking a way to destroy him, for they feared him, because all the crowd was astonished at his teaching." (Mark 11:15-18, ESV)

This is a living manuscript and will continuously evolve based on your constructive feedback (contact @ www.EPM-Mavericks.com or www.Tiger-Rider.com)

Proceeds from this book will be donated to Mother Teresa Mission (Missionaries of Charity) or similar missions.

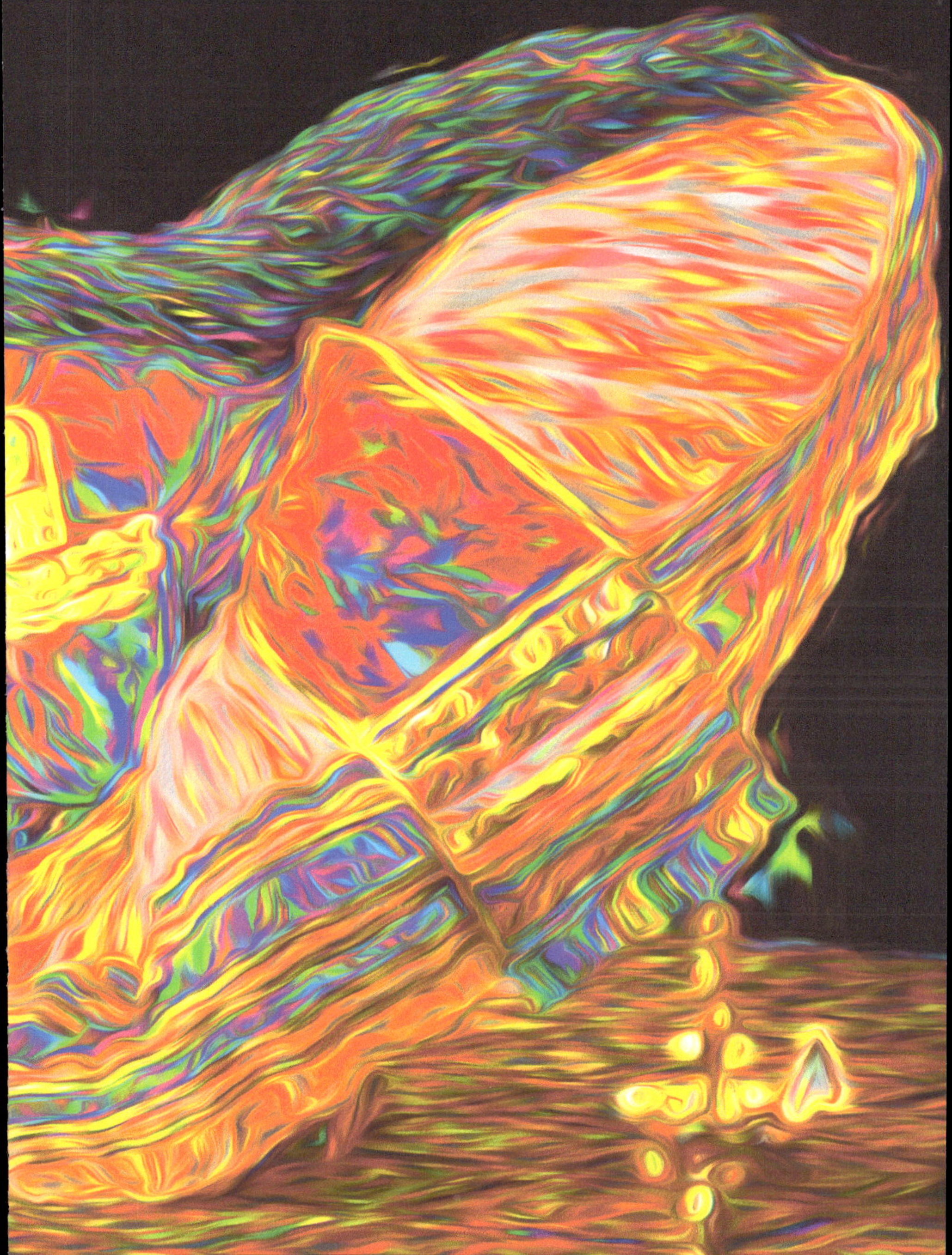

STRAUS & CO

“Unless there is security here at home, there cannot be lasting peace in the world.”

— Franklin Delano Roosevelt —

As I write this, there is *anarchy* breaking out; a civil *war* is going on right in front of my home in the heart of Chicago. Quoting a recorded call from the Chicago City Council, “it is ‘*a virtual war zone*’ where ‘*gang members armed with AK-47s were threatening to shoot black people.*’ *They are shooting at the police.*”

Meanwhile, in the mayor’s office, the City Council’s recorded strategy discussion that was intended to resolve the problem, devolved into a profanity-laden shouting match reminiscent of the Chiraq[1] banana republic[2]. I wonder what the future has in store for us if this boarding-up[3] can happen to my centennial home? Even one of the most exquisite and iconic ivory towers in the world (Britannica’s last headquarters), protected by a private militia, seems to be unsafe.

I took the *One Shared World* pledge to be an advocate and safeguard, not only of my beloved United States but humanity at large. I believe it is my moral responsibility to educate others about a predictive, preventative, and responsive infrastructure that might protect us from shared existential threats.

TABLE OF CONTENTS

ANATOMY OF THE BOOK

THE IMMINENT RISE OF THE MIDDLE KINGDOM

The Dawn of the Middle Kingdom

Our empire is endangered, and the existence of its enterprise subjects is threatened along with it. If we do not play our cards right, the next voracious empire (The Middle Kingdom[4]) will soon send its errand boys to collect bills from the US and over a hundred other countries that it has financially colonized since the economic tsunami of 2008.

The Gods Must Be Crazy

In the book's initial section, I tell of my tiger-ride through the distorted fields of reality; from the cradle of communism in the East to the catacombs of capitalism in the West. This is portrayed against the backdrop of Hernando de Soto's book, *The Mystery of Capital: Why Capitalism Triumphs in the West and Fails Everywhere Else*.

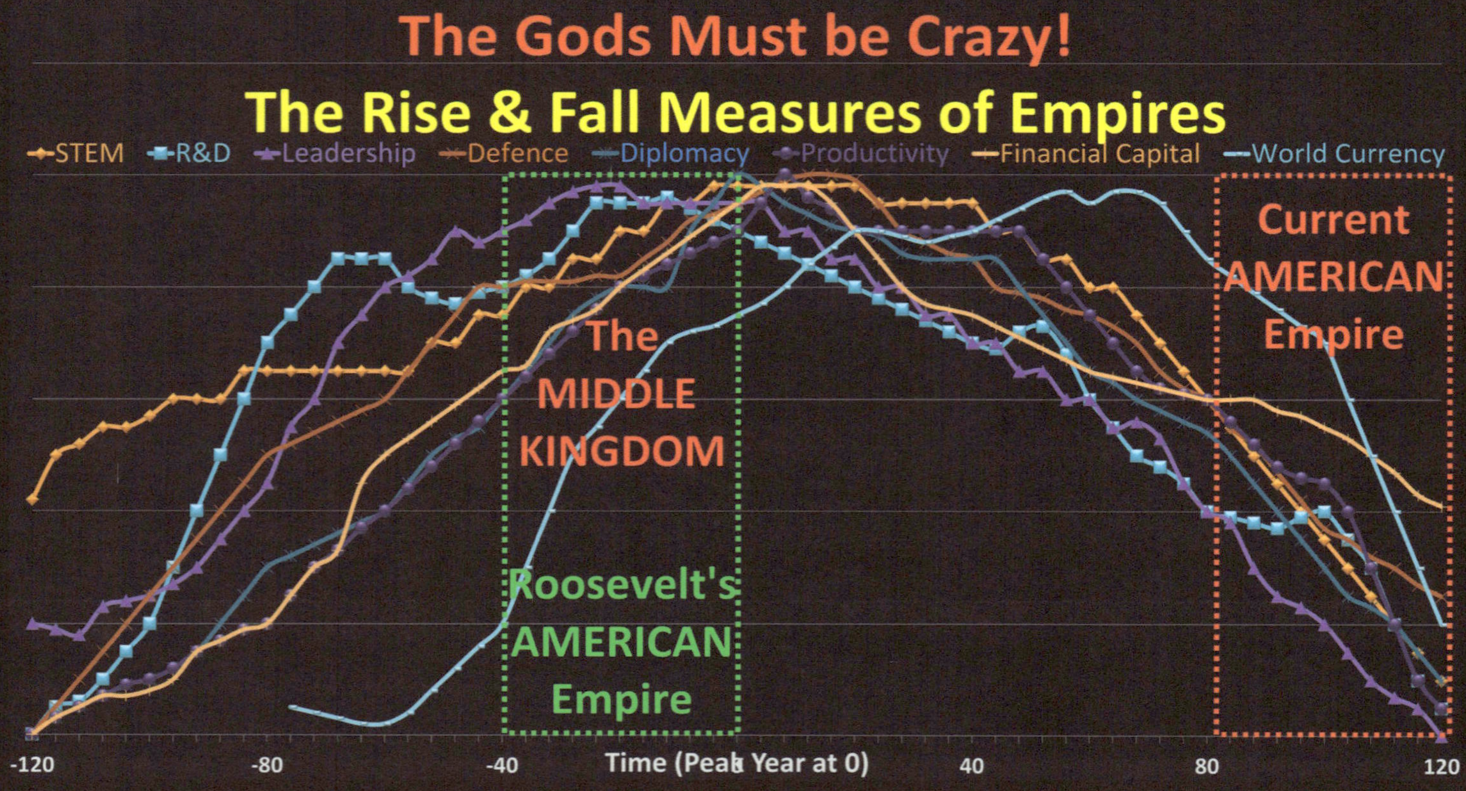
The Gods Must be Crazy!
The Rise & Fall Measures of Empires
STEM
R&D
Leadership
Defence
Diplomacy
Productivity
Financial Capital
World Currency
The MIDDLE KINGDOM
Roosevelt's AMERICAN Empire
Current AMERICAN Empire
-120
-80
-40
40
80
120
Time (Peak Year at 0)

A Proposal to bring back the House of Roosevelts

In the second section of the book, I adapt *The New Normal* from *Empire to Enterprise*'s perspective to explain how to save us from the impending Fourth Reich[5]. The survival of an enterprise is intertwined with the rise and fall of its sponsoring godfathers, the world's empires - as we have witnessed in the past five centuries, with the most prominent enterprises such as the Dutch[6] and British[7] East India companies.

★ ★

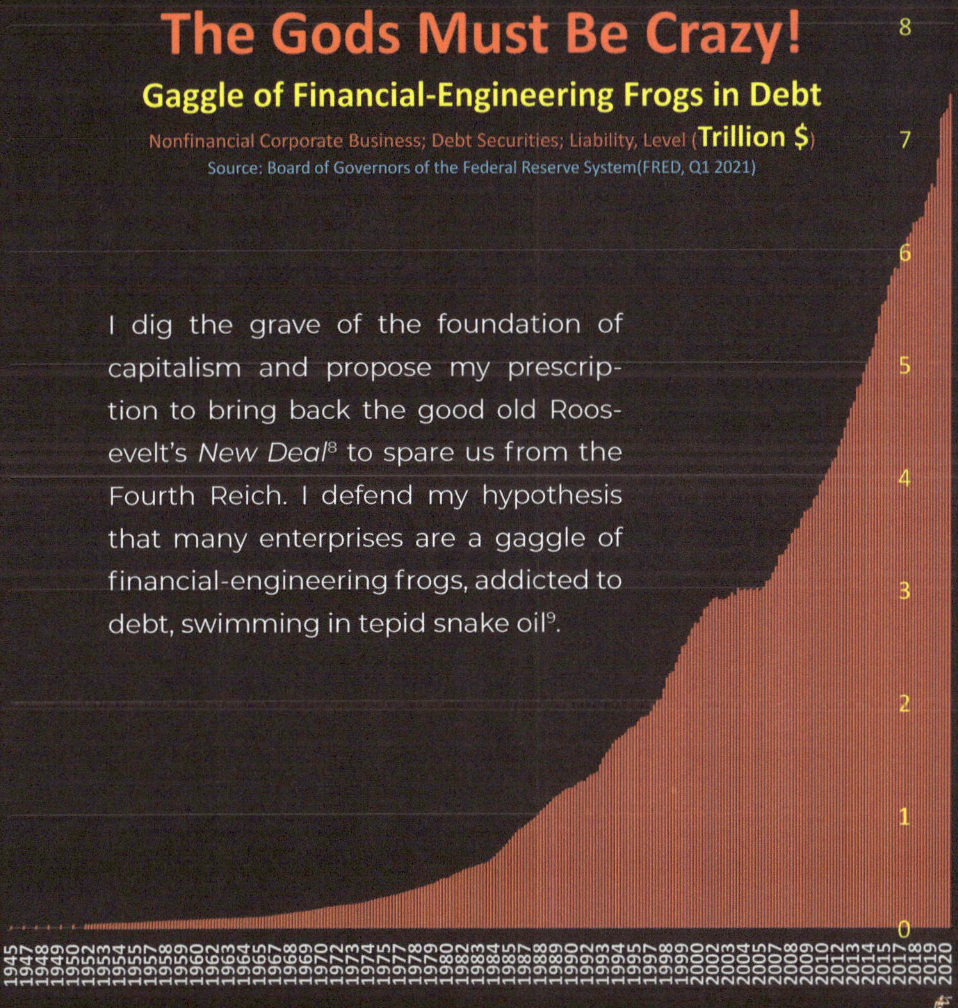

I dig the grave of the foundation of capitalism and propose my prescription to bring back the good old Roosevelt's *New Deal*[8] to spare us from the Fourth Reich. I defend my hypothesis that many enterprises are a gaggle of financial-engineering frogs, addicted to debt, swimming in tepid snake oil[9].

When the tide goes out, many of these enterprises will meet their sordid destiny at the hands of IP (Intellectual Property) vultures such as China, as shown in the chart below:

Ay Yi Yai Yi! We are in the middle of The New World Order!

THE DAWN OF THE MIDDLE KINGDOM

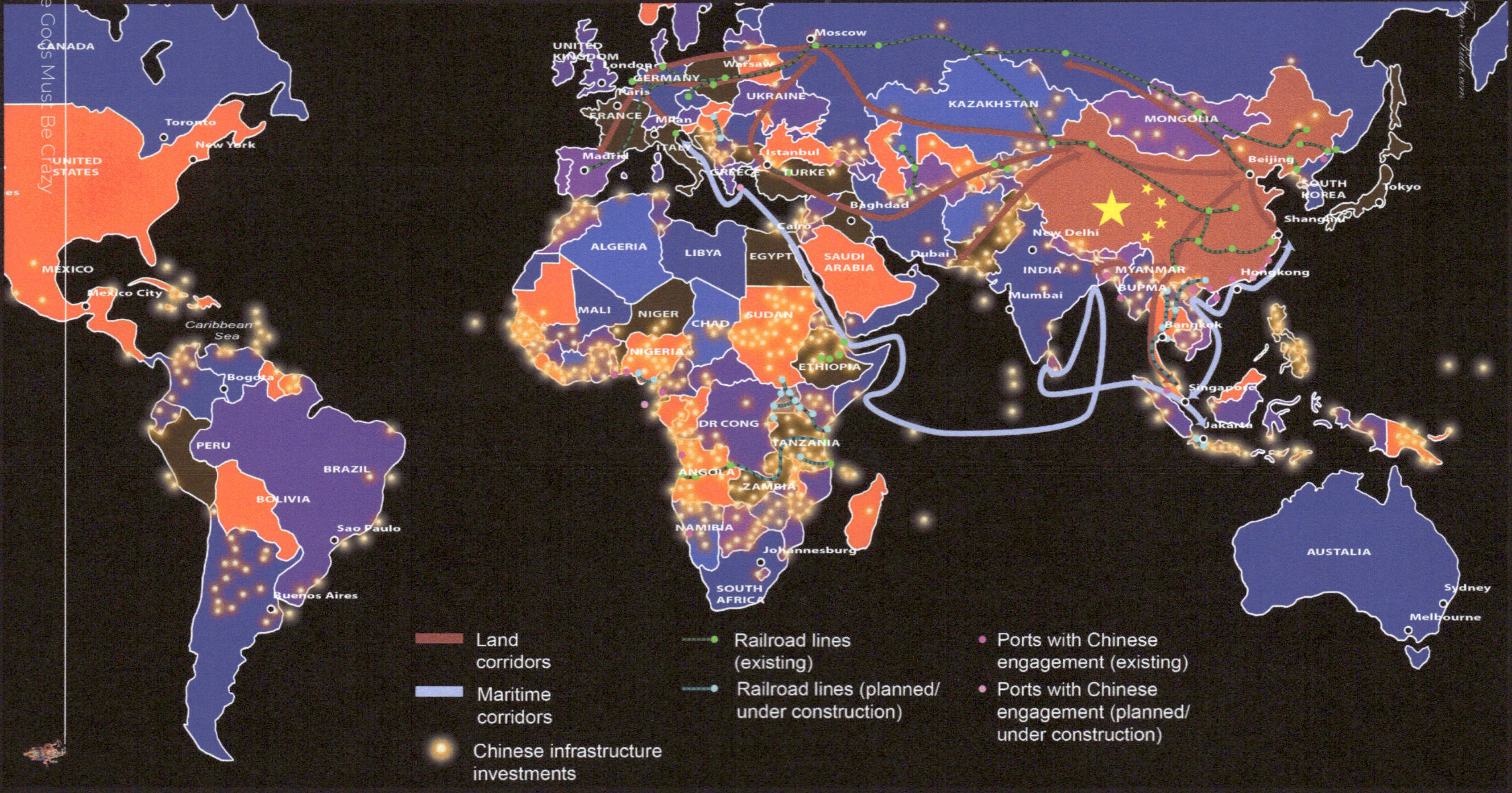

> *"The art of war is of vital importance to the State. It is a matter of life and death, a road either to safety or to ruin. Hence it is a subject of inquiry which can on no account be neglected."*
>
> Sun Tzu's The Art of War (476–221 BC)

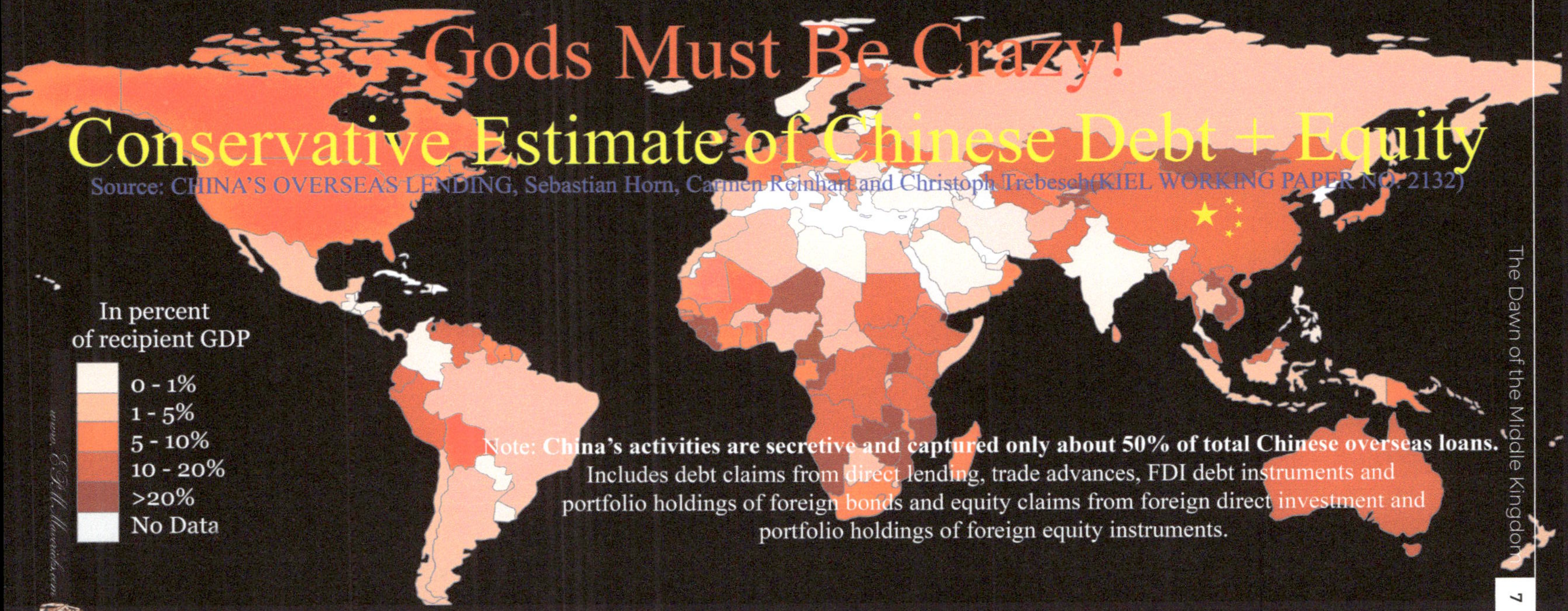
Gods Must Be Crazy!
Conservative Estimate of Chinese Debt + Equity
Source: CHINA'S OVERSEAS LENDING, Sebastian Horn, Carmen Reinhart and Christoph Trebesch(KIEL WORKING PAPER NO. 2132)
In percent of recipient GDP
0 - 1%
1 - 5%
5 - 10%
10 - 20%
>20%
No Data
Note: China's activities are secretive and captured only about 50% of total Chinese overseas loans.
Includes debt claims from direct lending, trade advances, FDI debt instruments and portfolio holdings of foreign bonds and equity claims from foreign direct investment and portfolio holdings of foreign equity instruments.

China, the Middle Kingdom, waits eagerly for us to misplay our worn-out trump cards so they may send their bounty hunters to recover the tab from the US and over a hundred other countries[10]. Under a governmental aegis, Chinese enterprises are effectively colonizing the world by financially influencing these countries with at least $10 trillion in debt-trap diplomacy[11]. The new generations of the Belt and Silk Road Initiative[12] and other high-tech infrastructure megaprojects are prime examples of the Chinese 22nd century Trojan Horse. Some of these parasitic and unsustainable debt-trap diplomacies may hide hegemonic motives and challenges to state sovereignty. They are bulldozed to support China's geostrategic interests and military dimensions.

"Compared with China's pre-eminent status in world trade, its role in global finance is poorly understood.... China's capital exports building a new database of 5000 loans and grants to more than 150 countries, 1949-2017. We find that 50% of China's lending to developing countries is not reported to the IMF or World Bank. These "hidden debts" distort policy surveillance, risk pricing, and debt sustainability analyses. Since China's overseas lending is almost entirely official (state-controlled), the standard "push" and "pull" drivers of private cross-border flows do not apply in the same way."

Kiel Institute for the World Economy (2020)

According to KIEL report estimates, as of 2017, China's total financial claims beyond its borders is more than 8% of the world GDP. Chinese holds bonds, and treasury alone are worth at least 7% of US GDP, 10% of German GDP, and 7% of UK GDP in each of these countries. In fact, China has a substantial foothold in the Eurozone as a whole, amounting to 7% of its GDP (this equates to 850 billion US dollars in bonds).

China can leverage at least 5 trillion dollars of debt claims towards the rest of the world, and the share of countries on the receiving end of China's financial "generosity" has almost reached 80% as of 2017. This dramatic increase is unprecedented in peacetime history and is comparable to the US lending in the wake of WWI and WWII.

Unfortunately, these 2017 conservative figures are now obsolete, especially considering the economic state of the COVID-19 pandemic-stricken world. The impact of COVID-19 on China's accelerating loaning and investing can only remain to be seen.

Once upon a time, American-founded institutions like the IMF and the World Bank used to be the big-hitting lenders of the world. Their lending method practiced full disclosure and had a certain level of transparency, ethics, and professionalism attached to it. This was especially prevalent when negotiating with corrupt governments and militias of resource-cursed countries.

The member states of the Organization for Economic Co-operation and Development (OECD) in the Paris Club and other reputed institutions like IMF and the World Bank would lend money more considerately with long-term concessional lending terms. Many of the Paris Club loans are in Official Development Assistance as defined by the OECD and have a grant element of at least 25%. These loans will often involve maturities of up to 30 years and almost no premium risk.

Gods Must Be Crazy!
Conservative Estimate of Chinese Direct Loans (2017)
Source: CHINA'S OVERSEAS LENDING, Sebastian Horn, Carmen Reinhart and Christoph Trebesch(KIEL WORKING PAPER NO. 2132)
In percent
of recipient GDP
0 - 1%
1 - 5%
5 - 10%
10 - 25%
25 - 100%
No Data
Note: China's activities are secretive and captured only about 50% of total Chinese overseas loans.
The debt estimates are based on loan-level data. They exclude Chineseportfolio debt holdings and short-term trade debt.
GDP data is from the IMF World Economic Outlook.

The Gods Must Be Crazy!

Characteristics of Chinese Loan

Source: CHINA'S OVERSEAS LENDING, Sebastian Horn, Carmen Reinhart and Christoph Trebesch(KIEL WORKING PAPER NO. 2132)

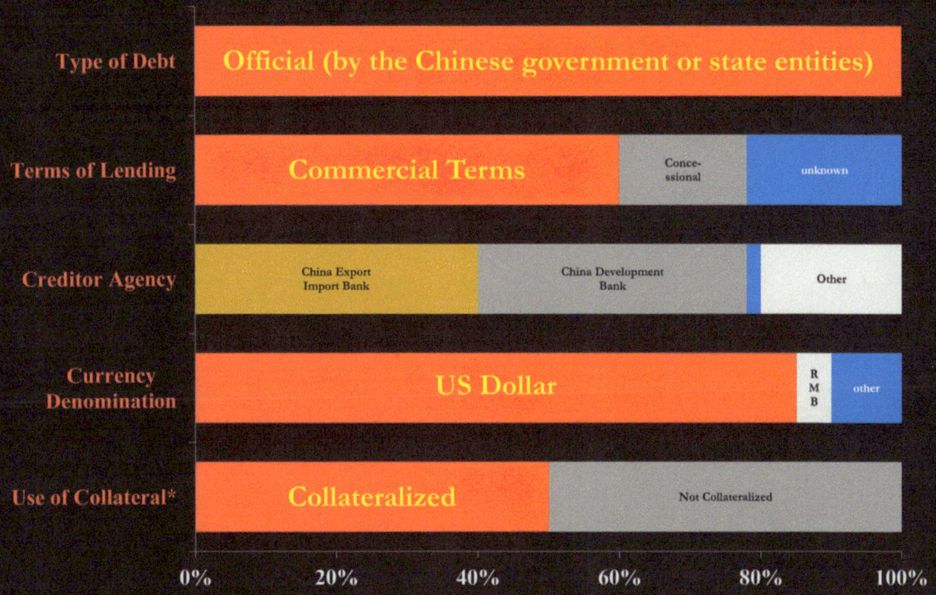

★ ★

It is also widely known that China is involved in under-the-table deals with less ethical governing bodies and militias of countries already struggling with a lack of financial resources. Furthermore, China's state-owned banks typically distribute the money directly to a Chinese contractor responsible for the project, rather than to the recipient government. This keeps the circle closed: utilizing Chinese contractor firms, with Chinese labor and materials, ensuring a more significant benefit to China and less for the host country.

These underhanded and closed-circle tactics are a form of debt-trap diplomacy that can quickly seize the ownership of assets. It's a trojan horse for China, which gains leverage and can enjoy financial colonization but leaves liability to the host country's taxpayers to foot the bill for generations to come. On average, the 50 most indebted recipient countries now owe debt to China, totaling close to 40% of reported external debt.

Chinese official lending is controlled by the Chinese communist party, AKA the government. Two-thirds of lending activity is channeled through foreign affiliates of Chinese banks in offshore financial centers. Next to impossible to track, these loans are backed mainly by collateral and done in the utmost secrecy.

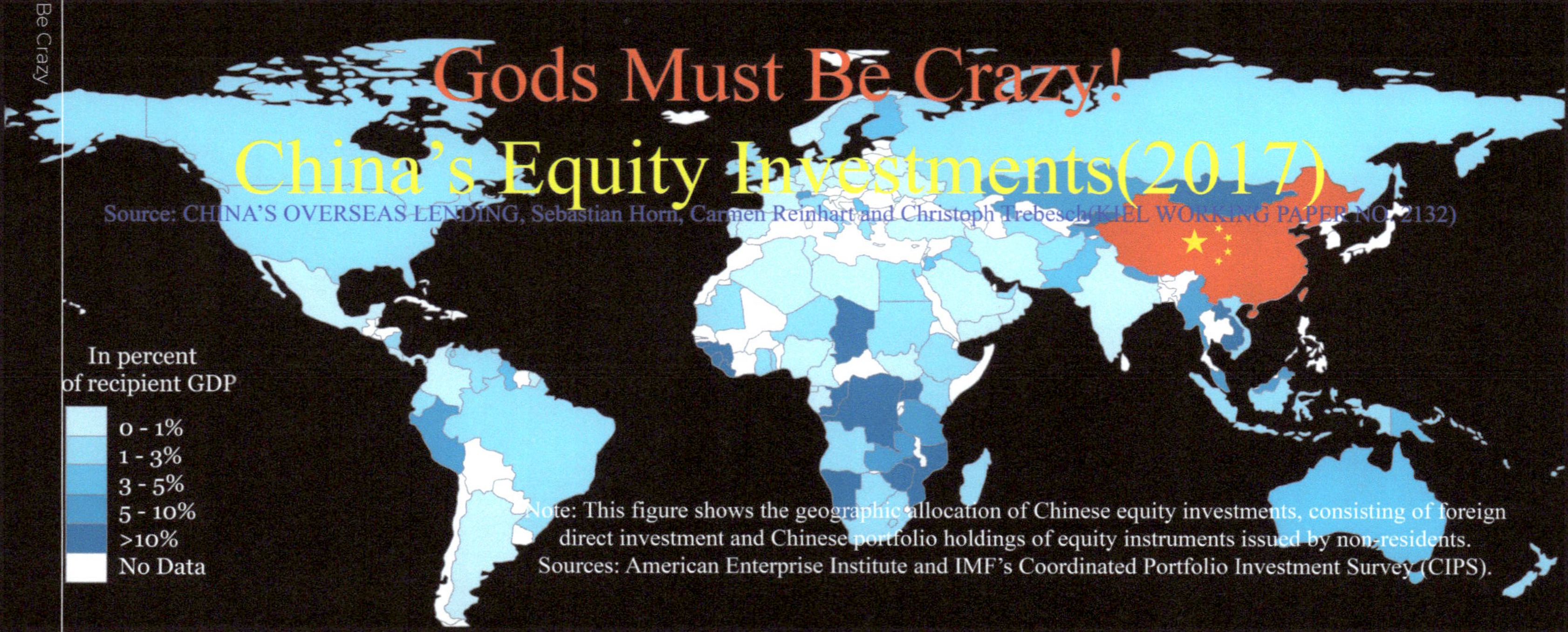
Gods Must Be Crazy!
China's Equity Investments(2017)
Source: CHINA'S OVERSEAS LENDING, Sebastian Horn, Carmen Reinhart and Christoph Trebesch(KIEL WORKING PAPER NO. 2132)
In percent of recipient GDP
0 - 1%
1 - 3%
3 - 5%
5 - 10%
>10%
No Data
Note: This figure shows the geographic allocation of Chinese equity investments, consisting of foreign direct investment and Chinese portfolio holdings of equity instruments issued by non-residents.
Sources: American Enterprise Institute and IMF's Coordinated Portfolio Investment Survey (CIPS).

Much of the lending is to financially poor but resource-rich countries being run by corrupt and inept leadership. As such, interest and principal repayments are often secured with those countries' resources. Unlike typical inter-governmental loans, these contracts are clandestine commercial loans with arbitration clauses. As a result, repayment amounts, default, or restructuring information are outside the public domain.

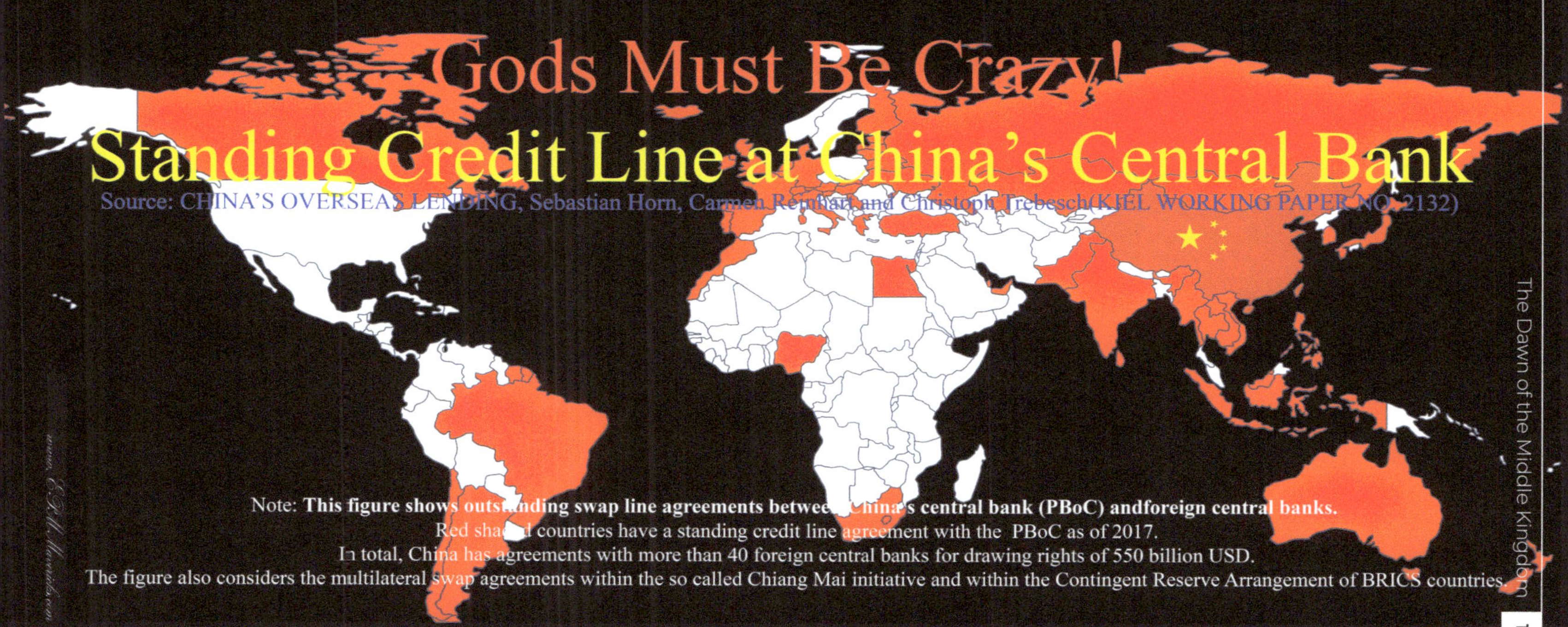
Gods Must Be Crazy!
Standing Credit Line at China's Central Bank
Source: CHINA'S OVERSEAS LENDING, Sebastian Horn, Carmen Reinhart and Christoph Trebesch(KIEL WORKING PAPER NO. 2132)
Note: This figure shows outstanding swap line agreements between China's central bank (PBoC) andforeign central banks.
Red shaded countries have a standing credit line agreement with the PBoC as of 2017.
In total, China has agreements with more than 40 foreign central banks for drawing rights of 550 billion USD.
The figure also considers the multilateral swap agreements within the so called Chiang Mai initiative and within the Contingent Reserve Arrangement of BRICS countries.

As an example, in the 1970s, a syndicated loan boom resulted in a wave of financial crises in the early 1980s. At that time, Western banks channeled a large amount of foreign capital to poor but resource-rich countries in Africa, Asia, and Latin America. It took over a decade to resolve the economic depressions associated with the string of sovereign defaults. With corrupt leadership and without much transparency or oversight, many of the same countries are now being preyed upon by the Chinese sharks.

Close to reaching the pre-HIPC (Highly Indebted Poor Countries) status, some have defaulted even prior to the COVID-19 era. The countries that have been hit the hardest by COVID-19, namely Latin America and poorer African territories, will undoubtedly struggle or completely lose the ability to repay their loans to China. Economic depression results in an accelerated commodity breakdown, and resource production has also been affected. With no money and no resources, the financial future is bleak for those China has an economic hold over.

It will be interesting to see what the Chinese post-COVID-19 neo-colonization strategy will be. How will it recover those under-the-table pawnshop loans, signed by corrupt leadership, and paid for in resources that now depreciated?

After World War II of the mid-1900s, the United States **donated** more than *$100 billion* equivalent (the US GDP was $258 billion) distributed evenly amongst economic and technical assistance to help the recovery of European countries. The whole world has flourished from the Marshall Plan[13], and peace and harmony have reigned for 75 years. It is high time that we lead the coalition to establish *new* Marshall Plans to rescue the countries economically colonized by China.

> *"It doesn't matter whether the cat is black or white, as long as it catches mice."*
>
> Deng Xiaoping, Paramount leader of China (1978 -1989)

Digital Colonization

For the past seventy-five years, our technology enterprises in the US have controlled a significant portion of the world's digital infrastructure. However, China is *extending* its "Belt and Road Initiative" (BRI) to its "Digital Silk Road" (DSR)[14]. China has signed DSR-specific agreements with numerous countries, and its infrastructure projects are a subversion, enabling Beijing to enhance its influence around the world without much competition. It is a digital backdoor for Chinese technology companies to torpedo western enterprises. Chinese telecom equipment manufacturers, Storage Infrastructure and Data Center companies are in the driver's seat. The DSR will also provide economic and digital corridors for the export interpretation of smart city sensors and data platforms, which can be potential national security threats.

There are four aspects to China's Digital Silk Road (DSR):

1. Digital Infrastructure such as data centers and optical fiber cables enable futuristic technology platforms like IoT (Internet of Things), 5G and 6G.
2. International institutions which set standards, rules, and regulations on emerging technologies.
3. Focus on eCommerce-related technologies such as electronic payment systems, cryptocurrencies, and digital free trade zones.
4. The Chinese strategy to "Make Middle-Kingdom Great Again" as part of the "Made in China 2025" initiative. To achieve this goal, they have invested heavily in the "Thousand Talents Plan"[15] (bringing back high-tech expatriates[16]).

State-funded financial quasi-Chinese enterprises such as Huawei and ZTE[17] are building most of Africa´s digital infrastructure. Their fiber optic cables have become the backbone of Central Asia's digital connectivity. DSR will give the Chinese Communist Party (CCP) leverage in the form of kompromat[18] to manipulate critical international leaders and enterprises, achieved through their access to sensitive data via harvesting and substantial data analytics capabilities.

China's Global Infrastructure Footprint

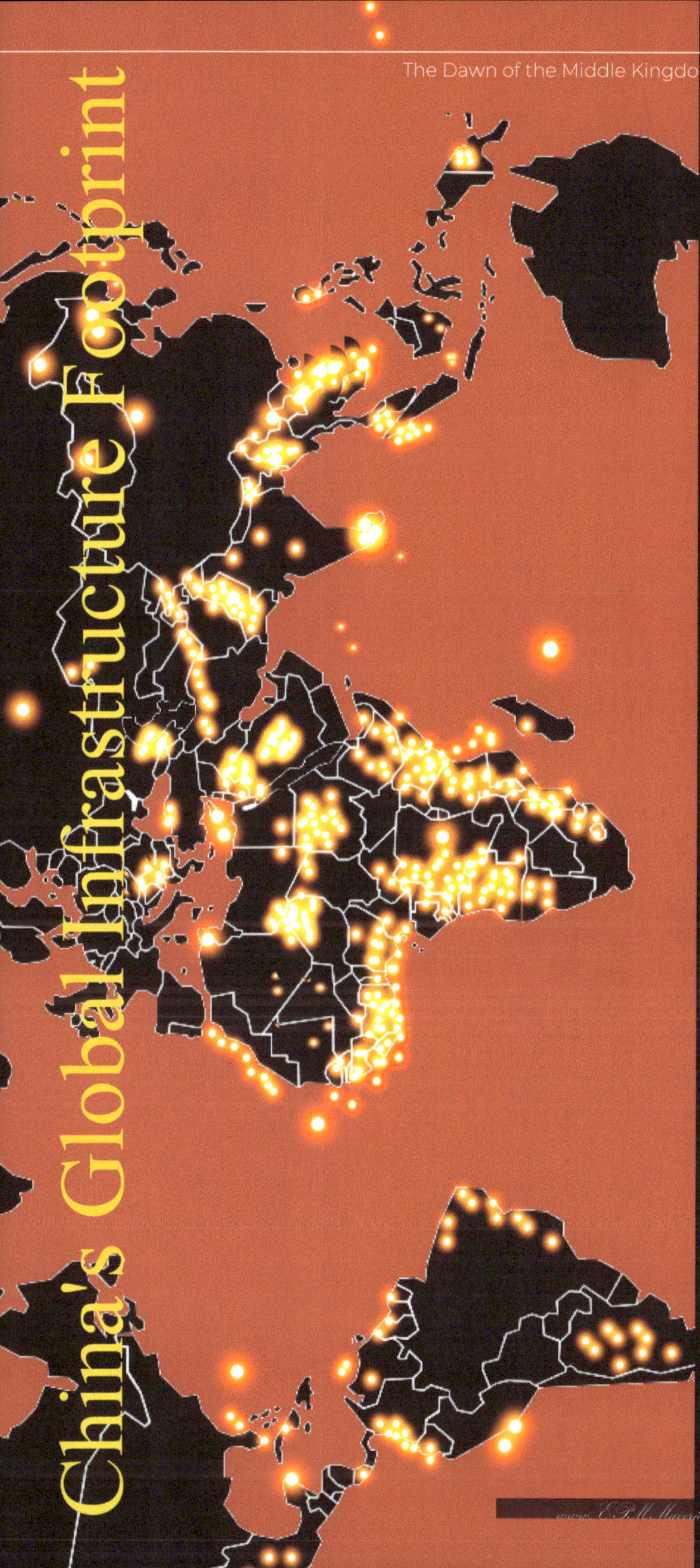

This structure will grant the CCP a massive sphere of political influence. They will thus set rules and standards for executing their political and authoritarian ideologies without regard for the host, their citizen population, and its sovereignty. Chinese privacy-invasive technologies such as facial recognition technology and cyber-espionage are already extensively used in many countries across the world for the policing of citizens[19].

Beyond Chinese eCommerce, the DSR enables telemedicine, internet finance, and smart cities. The most alarming aspect of this is that the state-controlled DSR can manipulate and harvest the data of its colonized citizens through quantum computing, artificial intelligence, and other cutting-edge technologies[20]. This information can then be used for China's benefit, not for the people.

"Don't you understand? The VC say, 'go away, go away'. That's 'finish' for all the white people in Indochina. If you're French, American, that's all the same. 'Go.' They want to forget you. Look, Captain. Look, this is the truth. An egg. [cracks it, draining the egg white] The white left, but the yellow stays!"

—— French colonist, "Apocalypse Now" (1979 Francis Ford Coppola film) ——

Competitiveness

The New Silk Road carried the primary purpose of expanding the sphere of influence and its investments in Asia through infrastructure advancements such as "One Belt, One Road" (OBOR) and institutions such as the "Asian Infrastructure Investment Bank" (AIIB). Chinese controlled AIIB has the highest credit rating of the three largest rating agencies in the world[21]. In 2015, this Beijing-based institution's initial investment was at least equivalent to two-thirds of the capital of the Asian Development Bank. AIIB's initial investment is also about half that of the World Bank. AIIB is a direct threat to the foundations of the World Bank and the IMF laid by the Americans.

The Gods Must be Crazy!

The Crocodile from the Yangtze

IMF 2018 GDP in PPP (Trillion $)

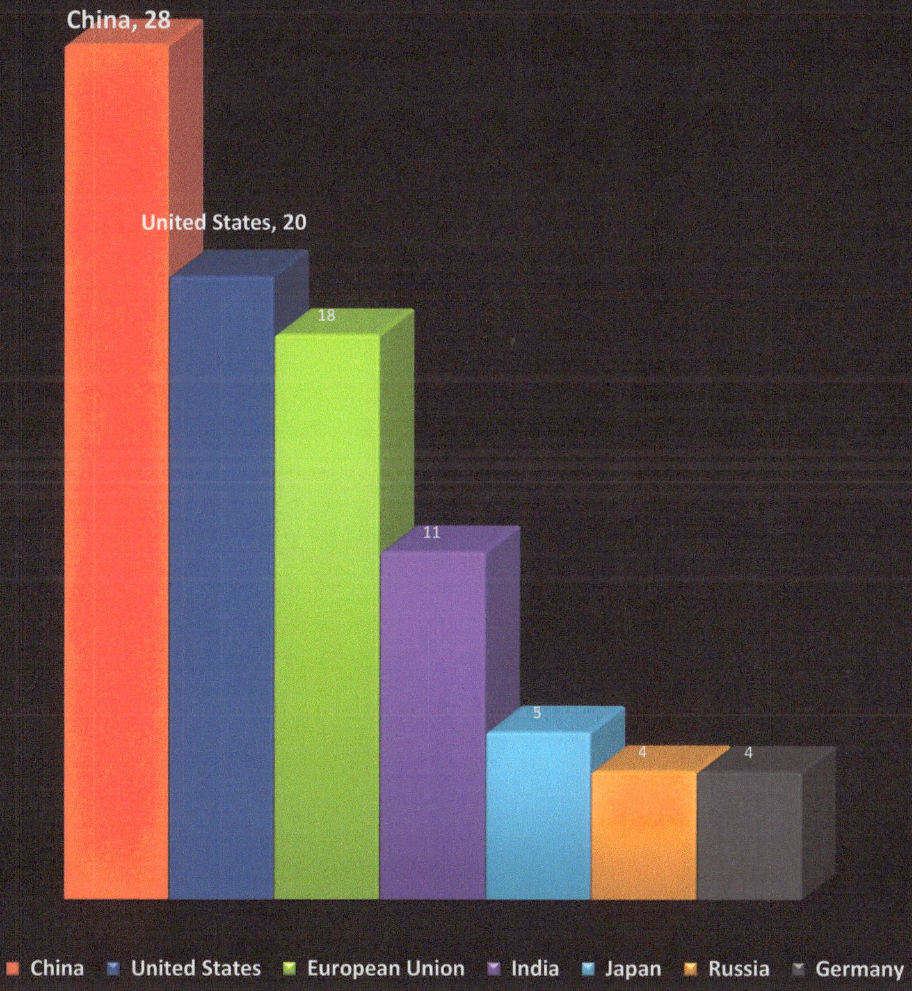

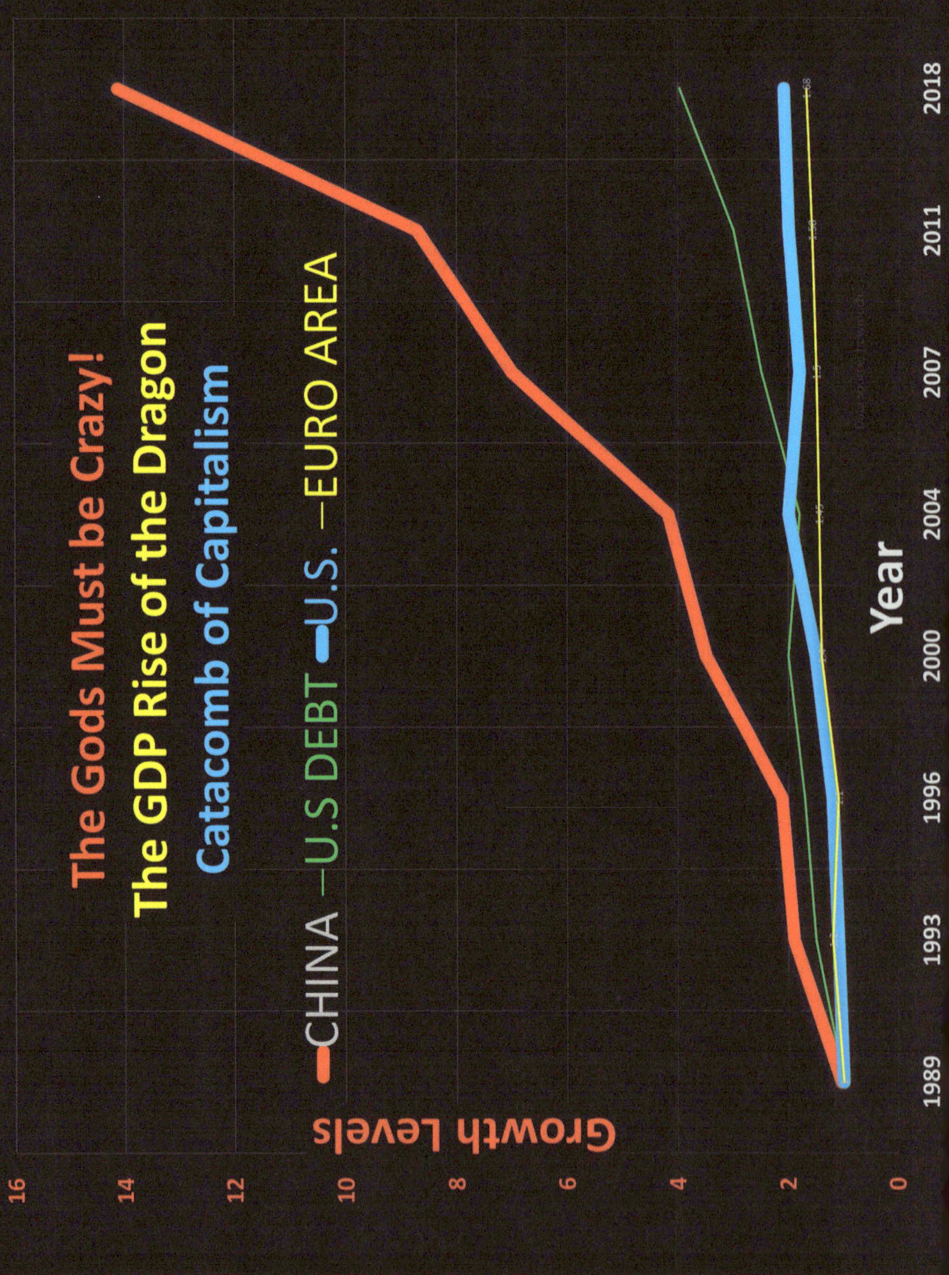
The Gods Must be Crazy!
The GDP Rise of the Dragon
Catacomb of Capitalism
CHINA
U.S DEBT
U.S.
EURO AREA
Growth Levels
0
2
4
6
8
10
12
14
16
Year
1989
1993
1996
2000
2004
2007
2011
2018

In 1960, the US economy made up about 40% of the world's GDP. Now, it is less than 15% in the "Purchasing Power Parity" (PPP) following IMF 2020 estimates. Meanwhile, China's GDP at PPP is 20% and persistently rising[22]. China's GDP has multiplied approximately fifteen times its size over the last thirty years. In contrast, the US GDP has only doubled. Meanwhile, US domestic non-financial debts are skyrocketing. This figure is currently at $80 trillion, while the US Federal balance sheet now has $7 trillion in unsustainable debt.

"The loss of income incurred by the private sector — and any debt raised to fill the gap — must eventually be absorbed, wholly or in part, onto government balance sheets.
Much higher public debt levels will become a permanent feature of our economies and will be accompanied by private debt cancellation."

Mario Draghi,
former President of the European Central Bank

There is already significant frustration associated with the pathetic lockout execution of COVID-19 containment measures. To add insult to injury, one of the financial consequences of Coronavirus is the acceleration of wealth transfer to the top of the pyramid. This meltdown in global financial solvency may result in unimaginable riots and anarchy, which I have witnessed in front of my home in Chicago; it could also trigger global civil wars. These international events could become much more radical than what we experienced in 2020 and may ultimately have a profound impact on the foundations of enterprises around the world. At the same time, China's enterprises are leapfrogging the old Western guards.

National Security

During 2017, we were squandering money on prehistoric military equipment and expensive personnel, while the Chinese military spent just 87% of the US defense budget[23]. They have been wisely and strategically spending to remove us as soon as possible, starting with their backyard in the Asia-Pacific region. China has over two million active personnel (vs. 1M US), eight million reserve personnel (vs. 800K US), and over 385 million additional troops available for the military (vs. 73M US). While the Chinese have intelligently studied all aspects of the US, American citizens are mostly ignorant of the world outside their nation's borders beyond the airports and fancy tourist traps. The United States population is susceptible to entrapment within their foreclosed ivory tower and green zones with a heavily fortified, "great, great, big, beautiful wall[24,25]."

The US healthcare system is ill-contrived, socially irresponsible, siloed, unhealthy, and the world's #1 healthcare squanderer (~$5 trillion annually). The sector is run by a gang of "medical cartels."[26] Pharmaceutical and Healthcare bandits have spent five billion dollars on lobbying since 1998. As COVID-19 has exposed, even under the Presidential Defense Production Act, we are hostage to China for our own 3M-made facemasks and basic personal protective equipment (PPE).

"In the US, 90% of all prescriptions are filled by generic drugs, and one in every three pills consumed is produced by an Indian generics manufacturer. India gets around 68% of its active pharmaceutical ingredients (APIs) from China."

— April 2020 study by KPMG and the Confederation of Indian Industry (CII) —

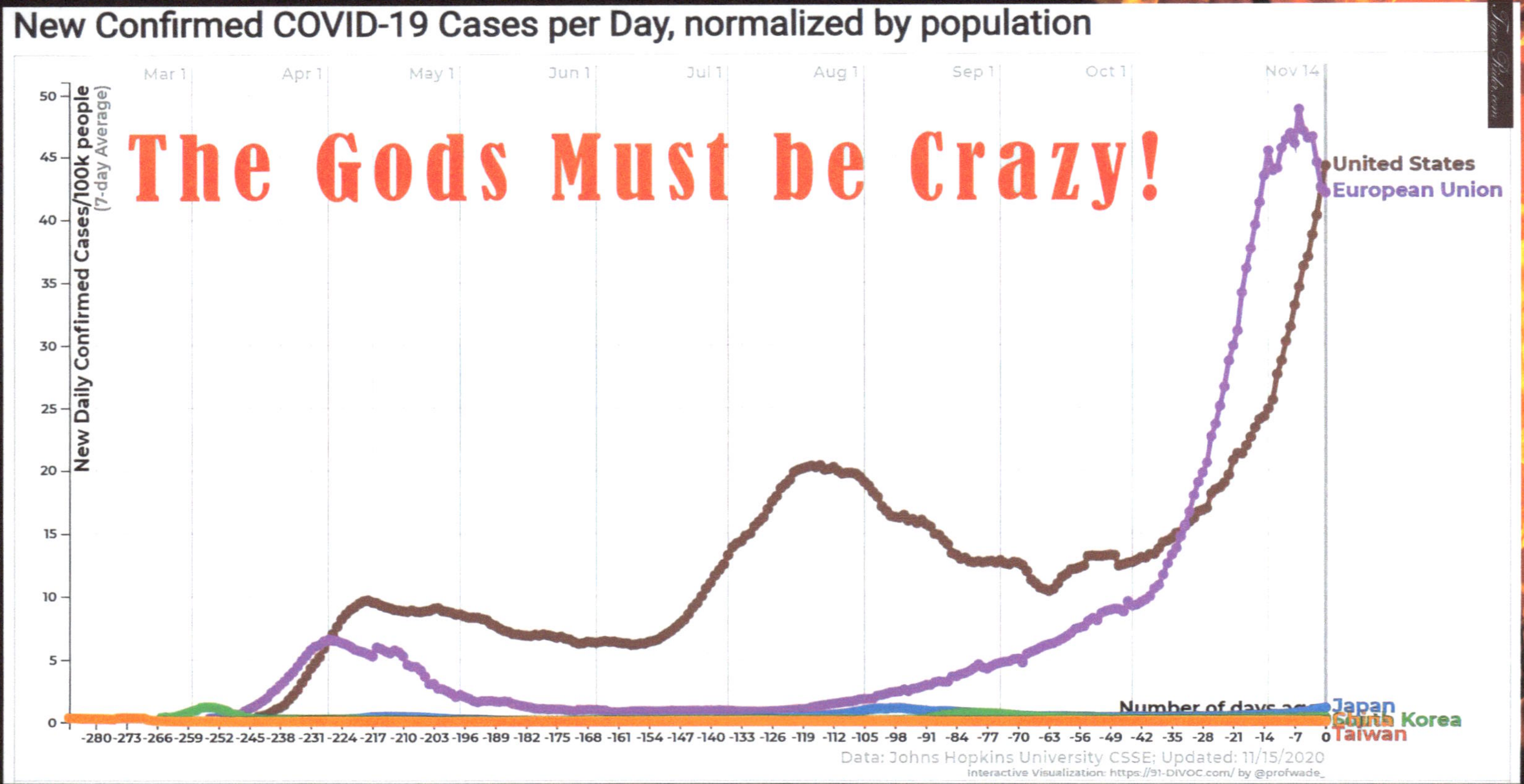
New Confirmed COVID-19 Cases per Day, normalized by population
The Gods Must be Crazy!
New Daily Confirmed Cases/100k people
(7-day Average)
Mar 1
Apr 1
May 1
Jun 1
Jul 1
Aug 1
Sep 1
Oct 1
Nov 14
50
45
40
35
30
25
20
15
10
5
0
United States
European Union
Japan
Korea
Taiwan
-280 -273 -266 -259 -252 -245 -238 -231 -224 -217 -210 -203 -196 -189 -182 -175 -168 -161 -154 -147 -140 -133 -126 -119 -112 -105 -98 -91 -84 -77 -70 -63 -56 -49 -42 -35 -28 -21 -14 -7 0
Data: Johns Hopkins University CSSE; Updated: 11/15/2020
Interactive Visualization: https://91-DIVOC.com/ by @profwade_

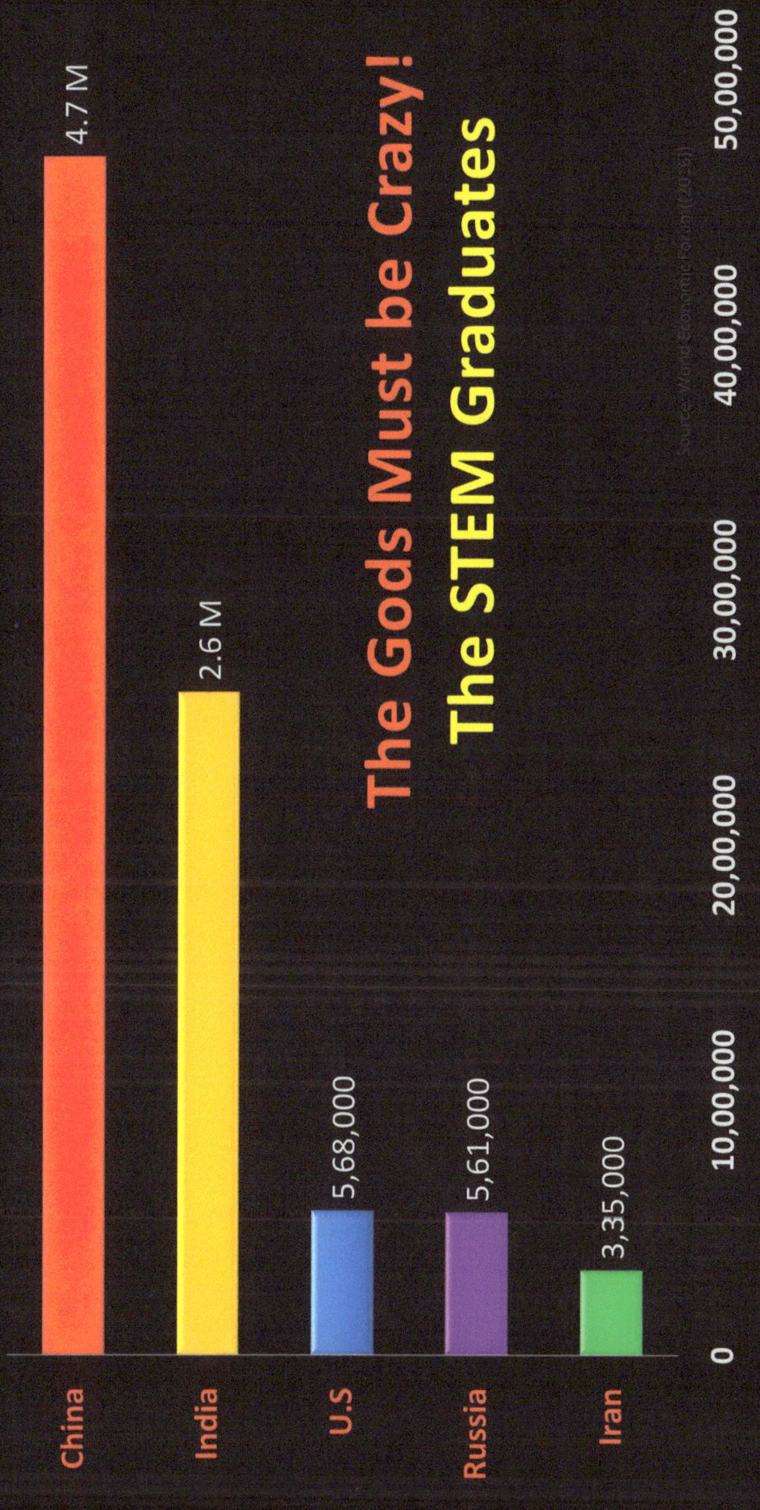
The Gods Must be Crazy!
The STEM Graduates
China
India
U.S
Russia
Iran
4.7 M
2.6 M
5,68,000
5,61,000
3,35,000
0
10,00,000
20,00,000
30,00,000
40,00,000
50,00,000
Source: World Economic Forum

Advanced Knowledge

According to the OECD, the US gold plate its financial budget on colleges more than almost any other country. This decadence, such as "the mania for athletic sports" without any ROI, is often attributed to educational value[27]. Unfortunately, the United States graduates a significantly smaller number of engineers annually compared to China or even India. China has spent 35 years building a patent system. According to the "United Nations World Intellectual Property Organization" (WIPO), the Chinese accounted for nearly half of the global patent filings in 2018, recording 1.54 million applications (vs. less than 600,000 by the US), led by telecom and computer technology.

From 2017 to 2018, the US sent over 11,000 students to China[28] for low-end education. In return, Chinese students made up more than 30% of all international students who study in the United States (363,000 students) for high-tech master's degrees, PhDs., and more in our prestigious institutions. China was building a new university every week, and 40 percent graduated in a STEM subject by 2013, twice the US standards. According to these estimates, the number of Chinese STEM graduates will increase by about 300% by the year 2030.

Advanced knowledge has historically been the driving factor in the growth and decline of empires and their enterprises. Knowledge is the foundation of a community, and it powers most domains. According to PISA 2015 report, the US has consistently ranked in the bottom 15th percentile of the developed world[29]. Sub-par education leads to a lack of opportunities and an inequitable society. This unfair treatment can lead to civil unrest, causing severe damage to the economy and its enterprises.

As a result, one in three US adults has been arrested by the age of 23. While the United States represents about 4.4% of the world's population, one in five prisoners of the world is incarcerated in the US. *Black men are six times more likely to be imprisoned than white men."*[30] These unfortunate statistics are the cause of protests and riots that occur on a consistent basis.

If we want to reach Real peace in this world we should start Educating children.
Mahatma Gandhi

(**Source Image Credit:** Unknown author, 1931)

Capitalistic System

A fish rots from the head down. The Supreme Court Citizens United ruling on January 21, 2010, was the final nail in the coffin of Roosevelt's Capitalism model. The Citizens United verdict opened the door for unlimited election contributions by corporations. Most of these contributions have been channeled by the secretive groups known as super PACs (Political Action Committees).[31]

Shenanigans perpetrated in our swamp (DC) and Wall Street enable tax breaks, bailouts, and bonuses to corporate executives who choke the goose laying golden eggs (their enterprises) via share buybacks and extreme financial engineering. From 2009 to 2019, American Airlines disbursed $13 billion in share buybacks, while its free cash flow for the same period was negative. All six major airline carriers invested $47 billion of the $49 billion generated on equity buybacks during the same period[32]. Today, unsuspecting taxpayers continue to bail these individuals out and the financial engineering horseplay will soon capitalize on this, turning the disaster into a bonus.

"The Capitalists will sell us the rope with which we will hang them."

— Vladimir Ilyich Lenin

Meanwhile, the Chinese government invests trillions of dollars in R&D, new factories, educating the labor force, and financing them to scavenge the fallen angels of the west (our businesses in financial trouble). During these turbulent times, even Saudi Arabian government vulture funds are on fire - selling shopping tours and gobbling stakes in crown-jewel US companies for a few million dollars. This whaling list includes our second biggest defense contractor Boeing, which spent $43 billion out of its

$58 billion cashflow on share buyback in a decade[33]. Our wise leaders are selling this country for a fistful of dollars. It is an issue of national security. They are willfully shutting their eyes and distracting the ignorant electorate by throwing rotten red meat to them.

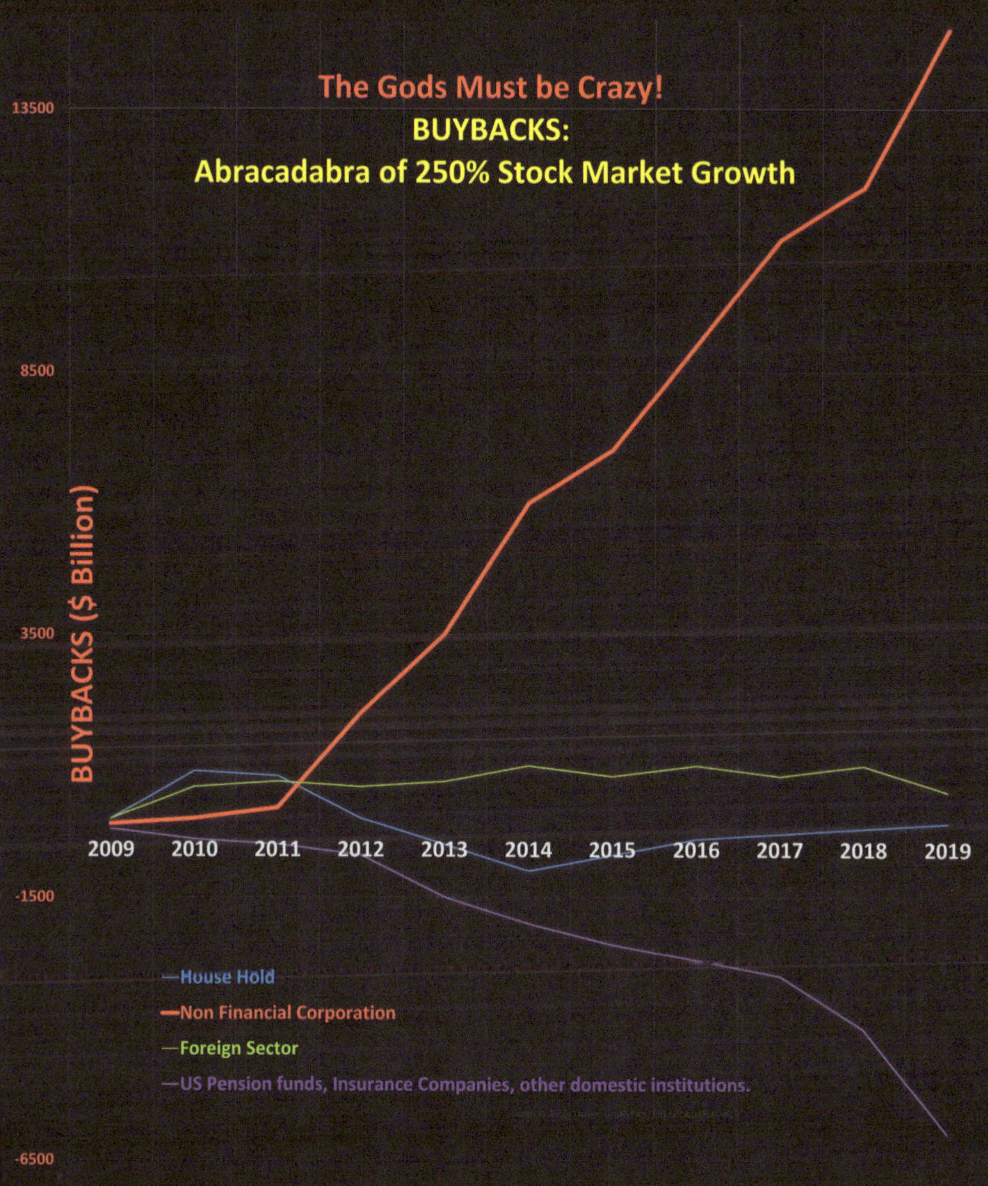

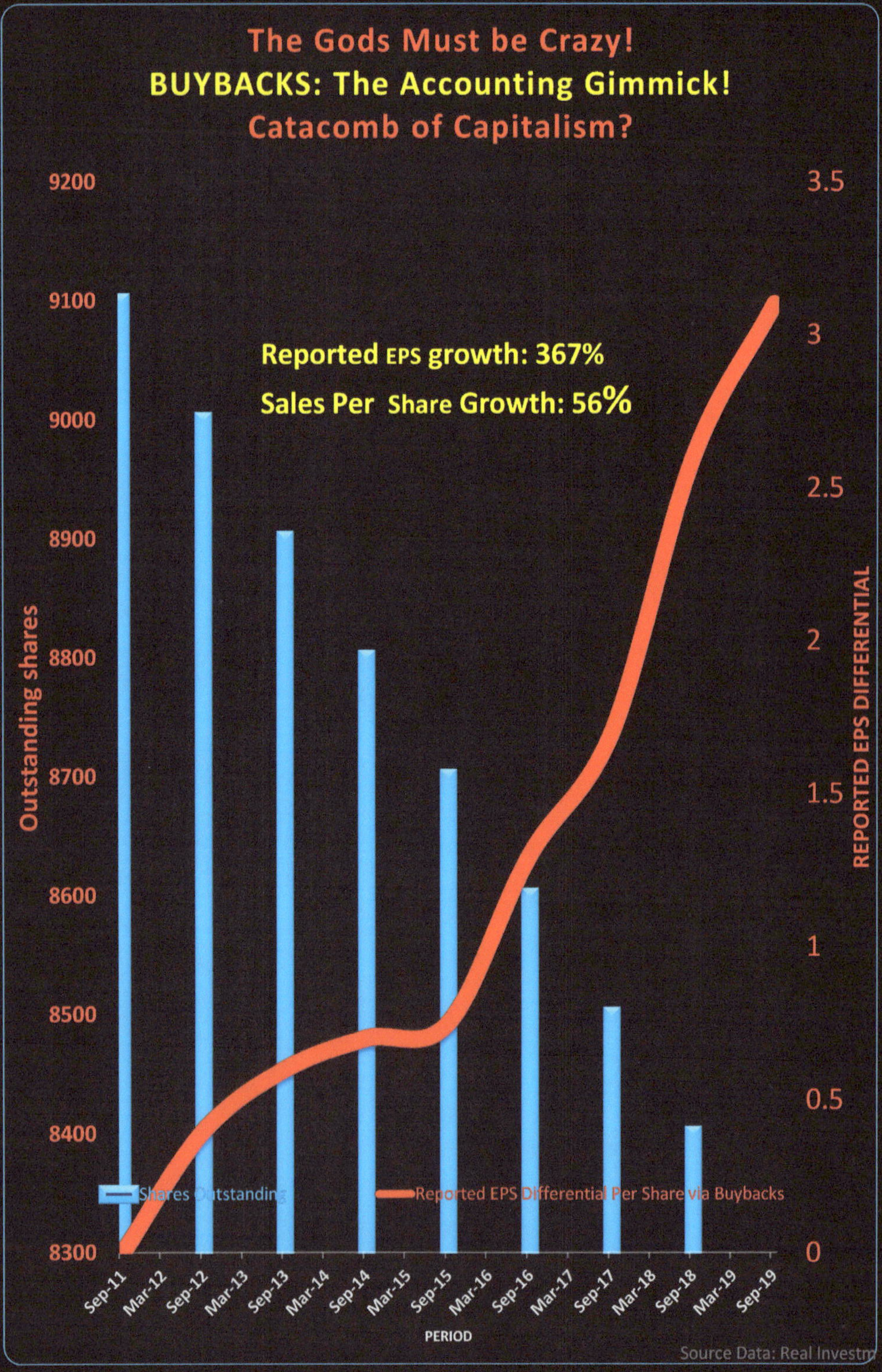
The Gods Must be Crazy!
BUYBACKS: The Accounting Gimmick!
Catacomb of Capitalism?
Reported EPS growth: 367%
Sales Per Share Growth: 56%
Outstanding shares
REPORTED EPS DIFFERENTIAL
9200
9100
9000
8900
8800
8700
8600
8500
8400
8300
3.5
3
2.5
2
1.5
1
0.5
0
Shares Outstanding
Reported EPS Differential Per Share via Buybacks
Sep-11 Mar-12 Sep-12 Mar-13 Sep-13 Mar-14 Sep-14 Mar-15 Sep-15 Mar-16 Sep-16 Mar-17 Sep-17 Mar-18 Sep-18 Mar-19 Sep-19
PERIOD
Source Data: Real Investm

"Buybacks are the primary example of a growing strain of incompetence amongst CEOs and amongst boards."

"On Main Street today, people are getting wiped out. Right now, rich CEOs are not, boards that have horrible governance are not. People are."

"What we've done is disproportionately prop up poor-performing CEOs and boards, and you have to wash these people out."

"Just to be clear on who we are talking about. We're talking about a hedge fund that serves a bunch of billionaire family offices.

Who cares? They don't get the summer in the Hamptons?"

"It would be better for the Fed to have given half a million to every man, woman and child in the United States."

Chamath Palihapitiya interview in CNBC

(Billionaire investor and the former Facebook Vice President of User Growth)

Elite Class System

Financial engineering by our elites and central banks, especially since the 2008 economic collapse, has created most of today's wealth gap. The lion's share of the credit goes to the father of irrational exuberance, Alan Greenspan, former Chair of the Federal Reserve of the United States, from 1987 to 2006. Interest rate-driven monetary policy, helicoptering money via quantitative easing (QE), and purchasing financial assets are prime examples. Borrowed money was free/cheap and utilized for buybacks, M&A, and various feats of financial engineering. This scene has resulted in over 250% of growth in the stock market in the past decade.

Unfortunately, only the privileged few had access to free/cheap money featured in the red portion of the graph. Despite trickling down, the vast majority (*see a tiny yellow part of the graph*) devalued the share of its pie. A few elites effectively privatized the profits and socialized the tax and interest liabilities for years to come. When China sends their debt collectors, it will be to the taxpaying majority stuck in the foreclosure hell, not the savvy elites in their tax havens[34].

The US is the only developed economy where the average income of the bottom 50% of its citizens has decreased in the past three decades. President Trump took advantage of this white, working-class sea of despair and backlash in the 2016 election. In addition to spilling precious blood, America burned over 5 trillion dollars fighting tribal religious wars in the deserts of the Middle East, which made a very few extremely rich. Each citizen of the bottom 50% could have received a $30,000 check had these wars been avoided. In contrast, the bottom 50% in China experienced the greatest three decades in 3000 years. About 800 million Chinese were liberated from poverty. In contrast, millions of US middle-class families have been forced to the bottom of the pyramid, relying upon food stamps and other government assistance.

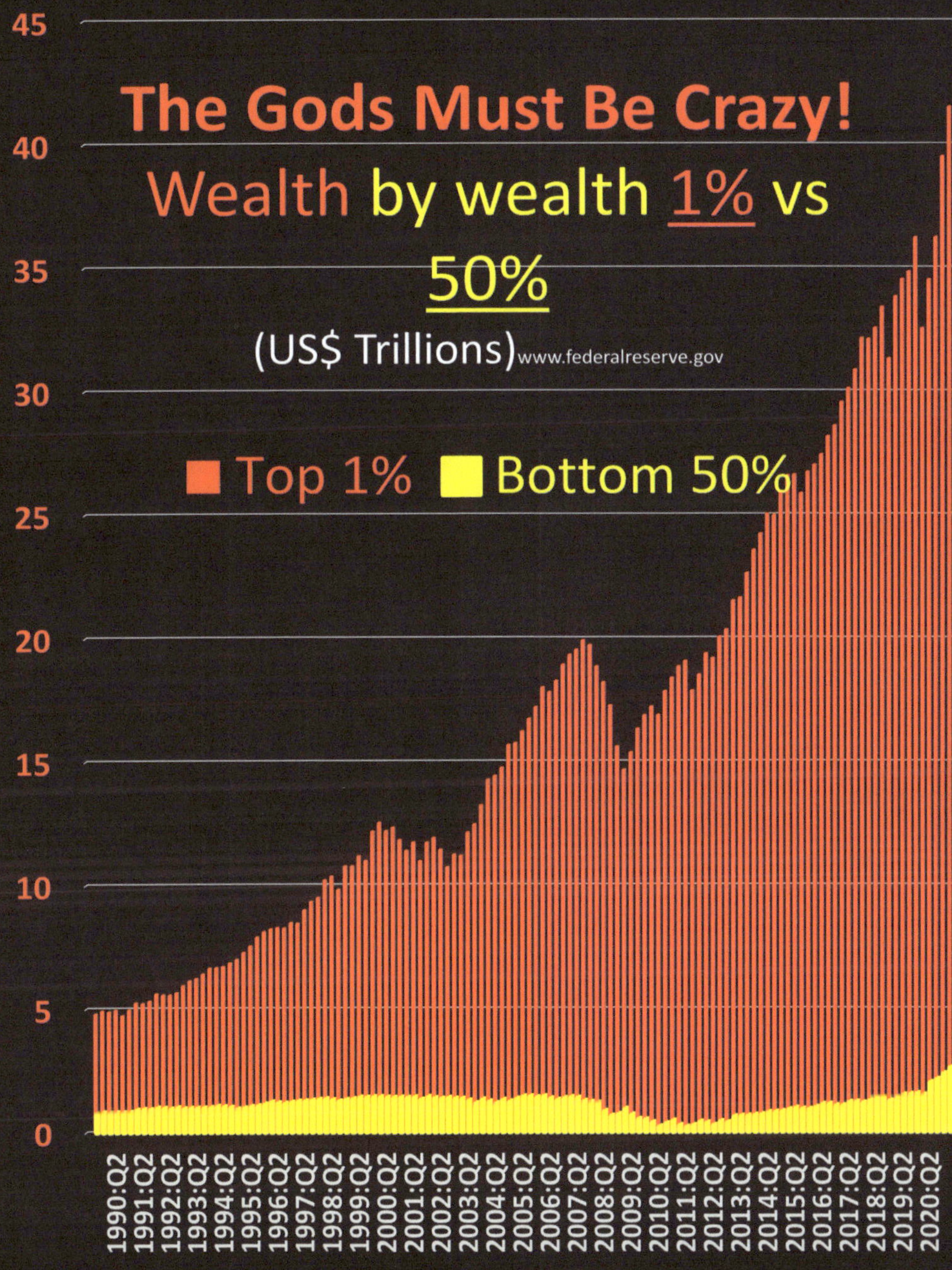
The Gods Must Be Crazy!
Wealth by wealth 1% vs 50%
(US$ Trillions) www.federalreserve.gov
Top 1%
Bottom 50%
45
40
35
30
25
20
15
10
5
0
1990:Q2
1991:Q2
1992:Q2
1993:Q2
1994:Q2
1995:Q2
1996:Q2
1997:Q2
1998:Q2
1999:Q2
2000:Q2
2001:Q2
2002:Q2
2003:Q2
2004:Q2
2005:Q2
2006:Q2
2007:Q2
2008:Q2
2009:Q2
2010:Q2
2011:Q2
2012:Q2
2013:Q2
2014:Q2
2015:Q2
2016:Q2
2017:Q2
2018:Q2
2019:Q2
2020:Q2

Roosevelt built a meritocratic society that became a plutocrat Zamindar[35], a system whose tentacles stretched deep. While China is run by the best engineers and is moving towards the meritocratic system, our leaders are taking advantage of the dissatisfied underbelly of our society and winning elections by throwing them bones from the garbage. The Chinese system cannot change the Communist Party, but the Party can strategically change the policies to take advantage of the country's best long-term interests. In the US, we can change parties every midterm or four-year election cycle; yet sadly, we remain stuck with the outdated close-minded "Hara-kiri" policies of a few special interest lobbies. The rule-based moral and ethical capitalistic system which the Roosevelts developed built a reservoir of goodwill at home and abroad in the past seventy-five years. Dismally, currently the US is draining the lake both at home and abroad with its draconian short-term policies.

The radical orthodox form of capitalism practiced today by wild financial engineers leads to debt traps, which contribute to economic colonization, populism, imperialism, fascism, uprisings, riots, revolutions, wars, conflicts, and anarchism. As we have experienced in US primary elections, presidential candidates like Bernie Sanders and Elizabeth Warren and others will unsuccessfully preach socialism (redistributed wealth while preserving democracy).

Dispiritedly, some extreme ideologists from the left will resort to communism (dividing most wealth almost equally), as witnessed in Venezuela, Zimbabwe, and North Korea. Most worryingly, many on the right spectrum will become fascist militia (autocratic state-controlled capitalism), as was the case with the Third Reich (Nazi Germany), fascist Italy, and Imperial Japan back in the 1920s and '30s.

"Black Swan" versions of extreme events such as COVID-19, which happen during (and exacerbate) times of vulnerability, serve to inflame the self-reinforcing downward spiral exponentially. A second civil war has been simmering since the 2008 economic crash, which resulted in massive wealth dislocation. The COVID-19 outbreak, Black Lives Matter rallies, and subsequent riots are gaslighting the embers of a slow-burning fire. If not managed correctly, the blaze will spread globally like the Arab Spring wildfire and spark the kindling of apocalypse.

Extreme Financial Engineering

Giving credit to the few Gordon Gekkos[36] in the Elysium[37], the vast majority of people are financially suffering. It is the culmination of the illusion that is so-called globalization and Roosevelt's capitalism. **There is plenty of blame to go around, and it starts with me.**

"The hour of capitalism's greatest triumph is its hour of crisis[38]*,"* and a crisis is a terrible thing to waste. The US became a capitalistic superpower because Roosevelt turned World Wars I and II, the Spanish Flu, the Great Depression, and other crises into opportunities by beating the British Empire, which lost its mojo. China is now enjoying a mirror situation. September 11th, 2001, and particularly the 2008 economic tsunami, offered us fantastic opportunities to take advantage of our undeniably supreme military, reserve currency, political goodwill, and myriad other resources.

But our lobbyists in the mire that is Washington DC have hijacked the opportunity, using it to prop up their Wall Street shenanigans (which kickstarted the trouble in the first place), instead of investing in our crumbling critical infrastructure.

Unfortunately, rather than taking advantage of the fantastic global opportunities, the BIG4 Consulting, and accounting firms, etc., took the parasitic route. These opportunities were framed as liabilities; the future and opportunities became cost centers rather than profit centers. They were well versed in the practice of extreme orthodox financial engineering. They persevered in flogging the deteriorated capitalistic horse for a few dollars, offshoring all the future capitalism to the east. These schemes include mindless benchmarking, transformations (IT, finance, supply chain, etc.), tax-effective supply chain management (TESCM), Business Process Outsourcing, contract manufacturing, R&D Offshoring, Restructuring, and more, created irreparable harm to the resilience of the enterprise. The end result is a dead enterprise horse.

Parasitic Vulture Funds, corporate pirates, and private equity firms took it as an opportunity to raid the few remaining enterprises with excellent balance sheets, sucking all the blood left behind by loading them with short-term, high-interest rate debt. Even when the raided enterprise failed, the private equity parasite firms pocketed their blood money thanks to the upfront fees and carried interest.

As opposed to seeing it as an opportunity to reinvest in their own enterprises, the leaders of our decadent corporates and their crony BODs considered it an opportunity to quisl the great balance sheets by share buybacks, thus enriching themselves. As in the economic tsunami of 2008, taxpayers rescued these zombie companies – the financial misbehavior in DC, resulting in privatizing the profits by socializing the liabilities to the taxpayer.

As per SBA, small businesses account for 99.7% of US employer firms and 64% of net new private-sector jobs[39]. In a few weeks of 2020 alone, 25% of small businesses have shuttered, leaving close to 40 million Americans unemployed. The clock is ticking on permanent shutdowns.

Being the suppliers of ideas and professional misconduct at these extreme financial-engineering scavengers, opportunistic IVY League business schools need to accept their fair share of responsibility for lynching the weakened capitalistic foundation built by the Roosevelts – Teddy, Franklin, and Eleanor. Many IVY league business schools' graduates, and high-end professionals chasing financial dreams, wind up in Wall Street or with one of the BIG4 firms. For a Few Dollars More, most of the crème de la crème engineers likewise wind up in this financial-engineering practice.

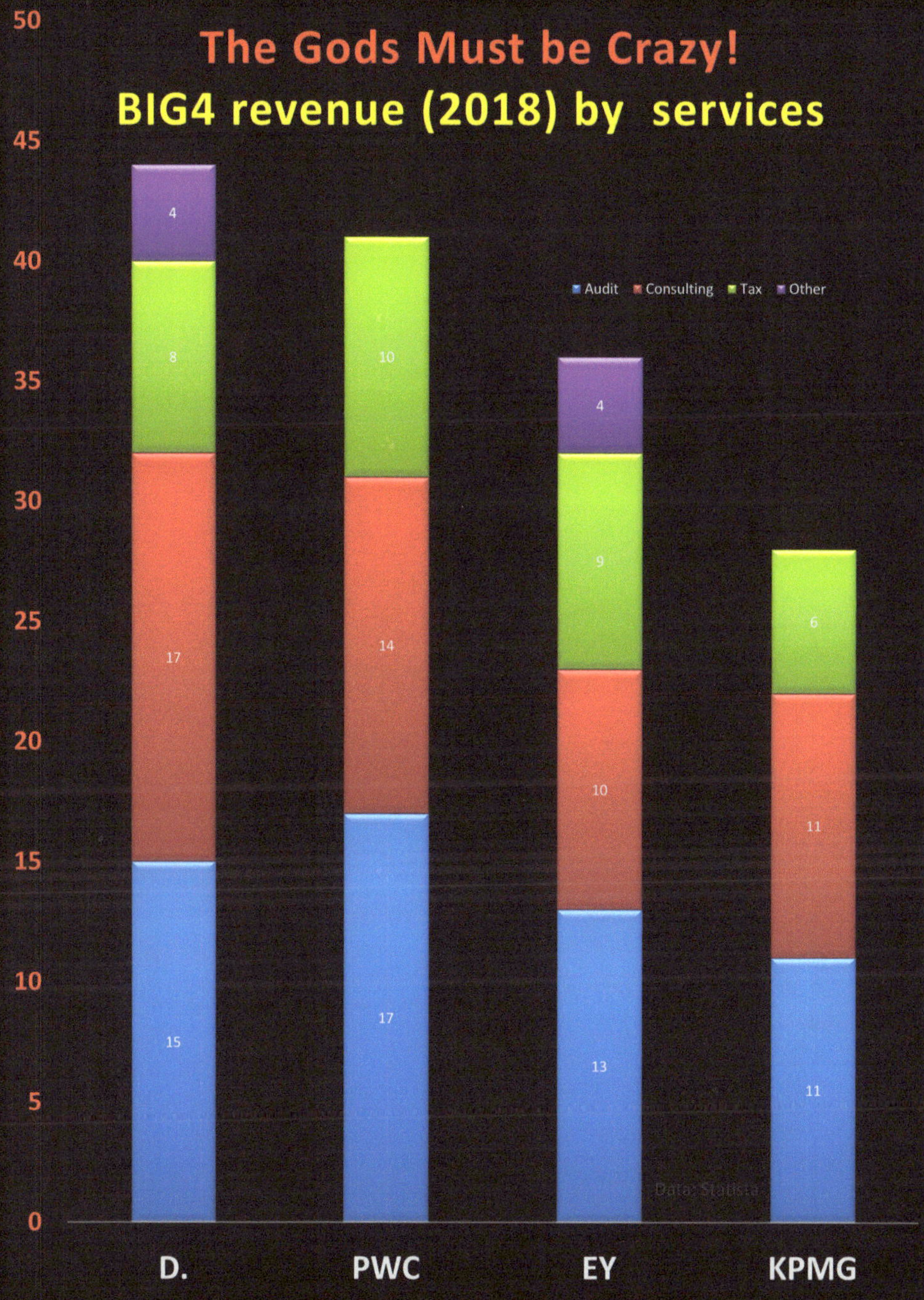
The Gods Must be Crazy!
BIG4 revenue (2018) by services
Audit
Consulting
Tax
Other
50
45
40
35
30
25
20
15
10
5
0
4
8
17
15
10
14
17
4
9
10
13
6
11
11
Data: Statista
D.
PWC
EY
KPMG

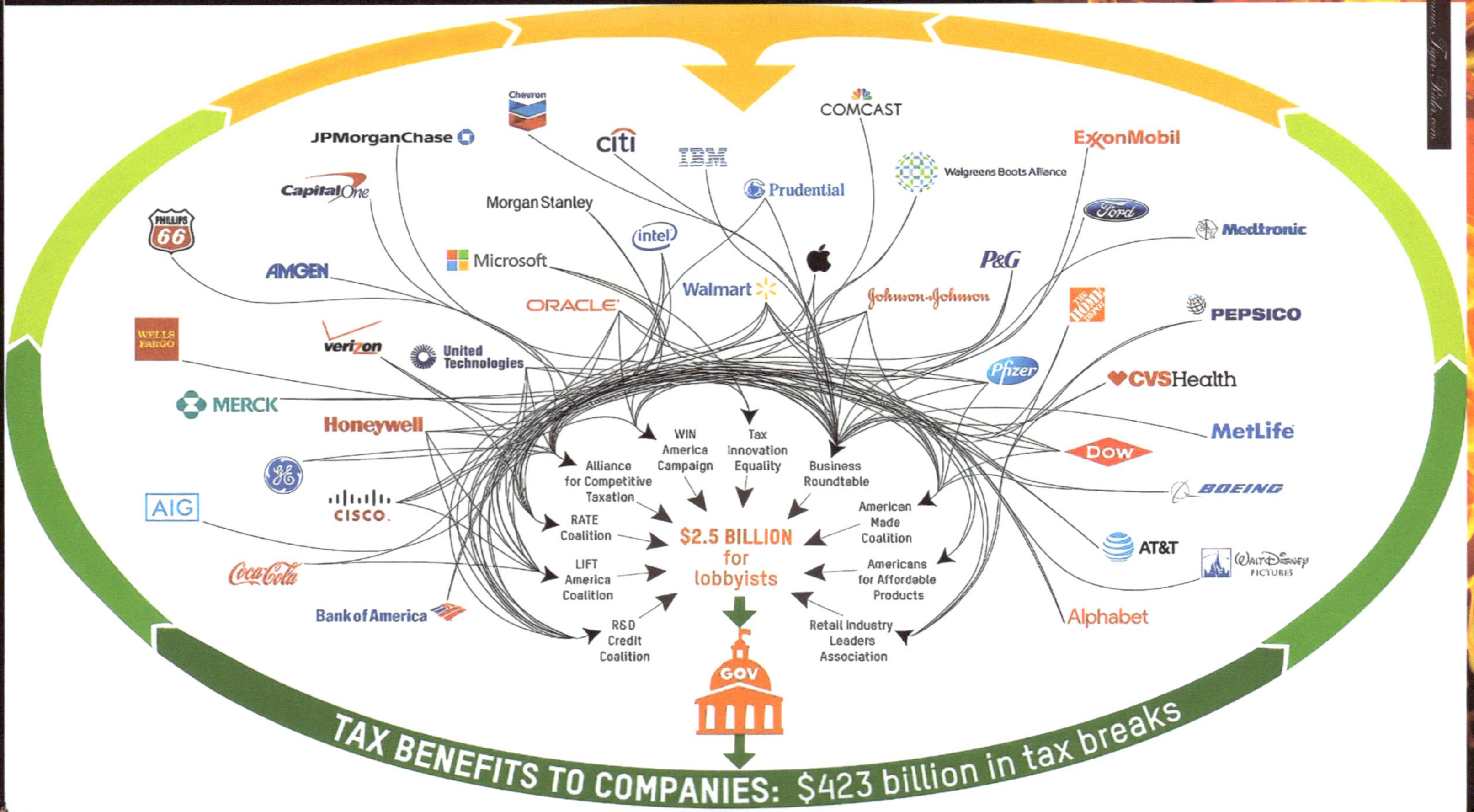
JPMorganChase
Chevron
Citi
IBM
COMCAST
Walgreens Boots Alliance
ExxonMobil
Capital One
Morgan Stanley
Prudential
Ford
Medtronic
Phillips 66
intel
AMGEN
Microsoft
Walmart
P&G
Johnson & Johnson
ORACLE
The Home Depot
PEPSICO
Wells Fargo
verizon
United Technologies
Pfizer
CVSHealth
MERCK
Honeywell
MetLife
Dow
cisco
AIG
BOEING
AT&T
Walt Disney Pictures
Coca-Cola
Bank of America
Alphabet
WIN America Campaign
Tax Innovation Equality
Business Roundtable
Alliance for Competitive Taxation
American Made Coalition
RATE Coalition
$2.5 BILLION for lobbyists
LIFT America Coalition
Americans for Affordable Products
R&D Credit Coalition
Retail Industry Leaders Association
GOV
TAX BENEFITS TO COMPANIES: $423 billion in tax breaks

But *what good is Wall Street*? Much of what investment bankers do is socially worthless and potentially dangerous for the US and global economies. Other than toxic financial-engineering products, what tangible things do they design, build, or sell? Wall Street disconnected from Main Street. They brought the economy to its knees, creating *Too Big to Fail*, which socialized the liabilities (to the taxpayer) and privatized the profits. They created the derivatives and other WMDs (Weapons of Mass Destruction) and encouraged skewed risk-taking in a rigged market.

As visualized in the graph below, two-thirds of the revenue from the BIG 4 comes from audit and tax practices. Audit practices perform the postmortem of historical numbers and prevent trouble with internal and external compliance requirements. Tax practices also help clients take advantage of tax benefit loopholes, PO boxes (offshore tax havens), TESCM (Tax Effective Supply Chain Management), and other practices that may be toxic to the taxpayers. A significant portion of consulting practices consists of financial engineering. To what extent do our IVY league institutions greenwash the CSR (Corporate Social Responsibilities) and ethical future of Enterprise and America? Or are they only capable of being termites eating away at its foundation?

> ***"From 2009-2015, the 50 biggest US companies got more than $423 billion in tax breaks and spent more than $2.5 billion on lobbying Congress to boost their bottom line even further."***
>
> — Oxfam America

Elysium[40]

So, our parasites crashed the capitalistic foundation architected by Roosevelt. As a result, we are experiencing the demise of the nation-state. In its place, we are witnessing the spectacular rise of a new class of 'Elysium-on-Steroids' hacking the collapsed foundations of Roosevelt's capitalistic system.

By stifling innovation and hijacking democracy, groups like FAANG (Facebook, Amazon, Apple, Netflix, and Google) are becoming the most dangerous cartels in the world. And with a combined market capitalization of around $5 trillion, they are threatening the very foundations of civilization.

FAANGM (Facebook, Amazon, Apple, Netflix, Google, and Microsoft) has added a trillion dollars in market capitalization just this year alone. That is more than the entire market value of the S&P 500 energy sector. Meanwhile, the real economy is collapsing. While Wall Street and the Tech-Titans were having the blast of their lifetimes, the misery ensued on the main street as it saw its worst quarter in at least 145 years.

A quarter of the world's citizens are active users of Facebook. It is arguable that they even got the recent past US President elected. In a memo, Facebook VP Andrew Bosworth wrote that the Trump Campaign's use of Facebook's advertising tools was responsible for Donald Trump's win in the 2016 presidential election[41]. It may even happen again. It will be interesting to see the US dollar's fate when Facebook colonizes its citizens with their Libra (cryptocurrency) Electro-Dollar.

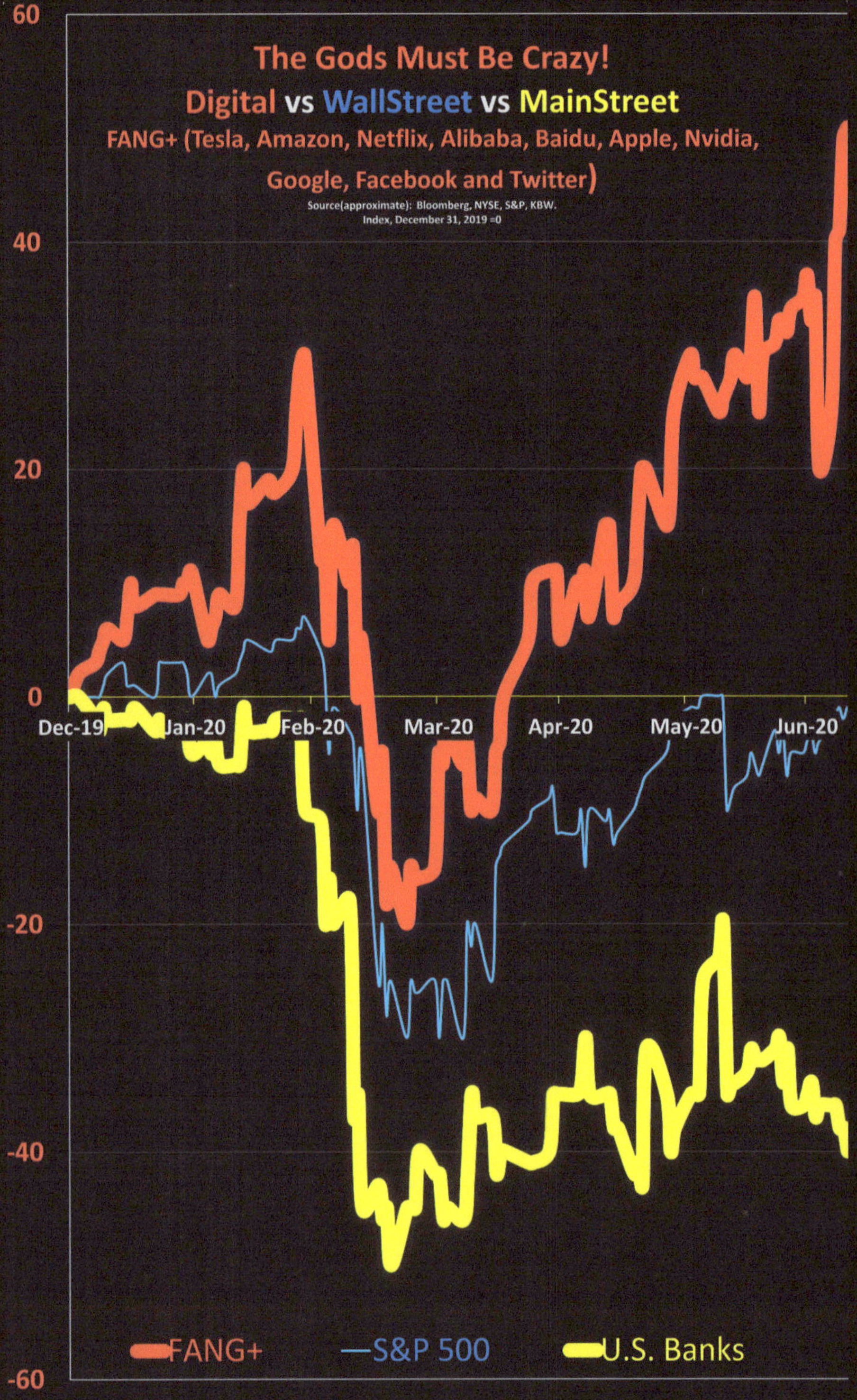
The Gods Must Be Crazy!
Digital vs WallStreet vs MainStreet
FANG+ (Tesla, Amazon, Netflix, Alibaba, Baidu, Apple, Nvidia,
Google, Facebook and Twitter)
Source(approximate): Bloomberg, NYSE, S&P, KBW.
Index, December 31, 2019 =0
60
40
20
0
-20
-40
-60
Dec-19
Jan-20
Feb-20
Mar-20
Apr-20
May-20
Jun-20
FANG+
S&P 500
U.S. Banks

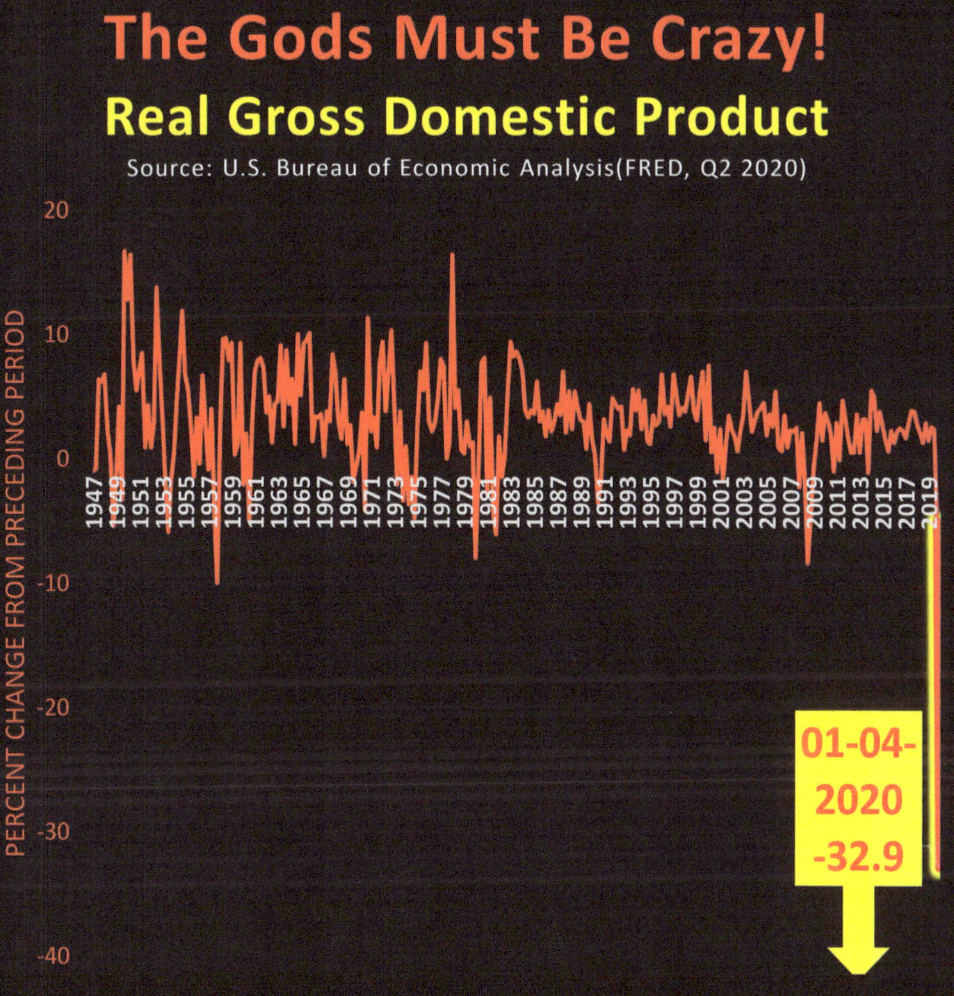
The Gods Must Be Crazy!
Real Gross Domestic Product
Source: U.S. Bureau of Economic Analysis(FRED, Q2 2020)
PERCENT CHANGE FROM PRECEDING PERIOD
20
10
0
-10
-20
-30
-40
1947
1949
1951
1953
1955
1957
1959
1961
1963
1965
1967
1969
1971
1973
1975
1977
1979
1981
1983
1985
1987
1989
1991
1993
1995
1997
1999
2001
2003
2005
2007
2009
2011
2013
2015
2017
2019
01-04-
2020
-32.9

"No civil discourse, no cooperation; misinformation, mistruth. And it's not an American problem — this is not about Russian ads. This is a global problem.

I think we have created tools that are ripping apart the social fabric of how society works. The short-term, dopamine-driven feedback loops we have created are destroying how society works. You are being programmed.

"I feel tremendous guilt. In the back, deep, deep recesses of our minds, we kind of knew something bad could happen."

Chamath Palihapitiya

(Billionaire investor and the former Facebook Vice President of User Growth)

Viva la Wall Street!

Once upon a time, New York was the world's financial center because the US was economically at the top of the world. China created its business center out of Shanghai, and it has already begun toppling US influence. After peaking in the late 1990s, the number of public corporations in the US has steadily declined. Thanks to private equity, mergers and acquisitions, as well as capital outflows, it shrank from over 7,000 companies to less than 3,000. Meanwhile, the Chinese stock market grew from *zero* to around 4,000 companies, in addition to the 2,500 listed companies in Hong Kong.

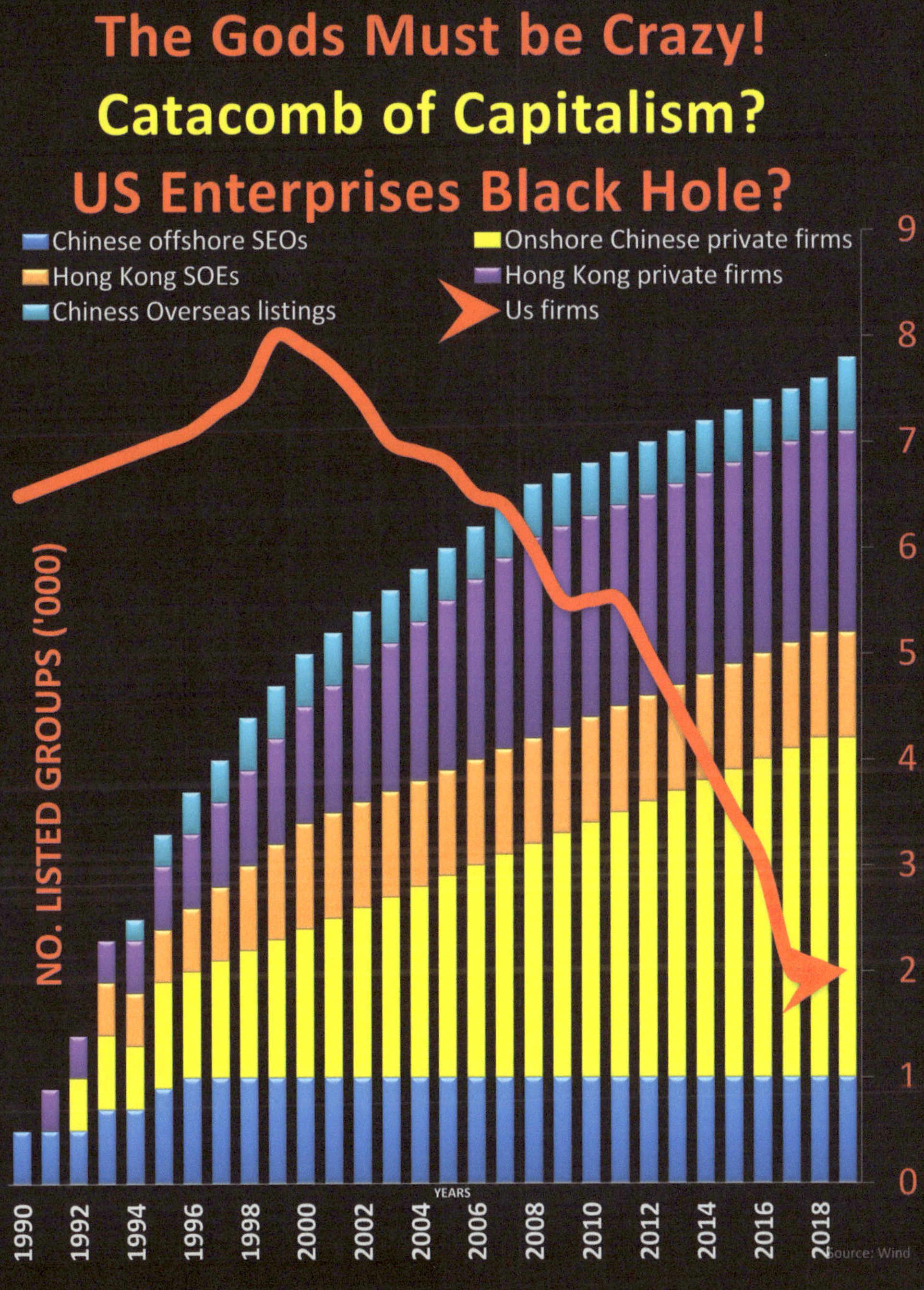

The Gods Must be Crazy!
Catacomb of Capitalism?
US Enterprises Black Hole?
Chinese offshore SEOs
Hong Kong SOEs
Chiness Overseas listings
Onshore Chinese private firms
Hong Kong private firms
Us firms
NO. LISTED GROUPS ('000)
YEARS
1990
1992
1994
1996
1998
2000
2002
2004
2006
2008
2010
2012
2014
2016
2018
0
1
2
3
4
5
6
7
8
9
Source: Wind

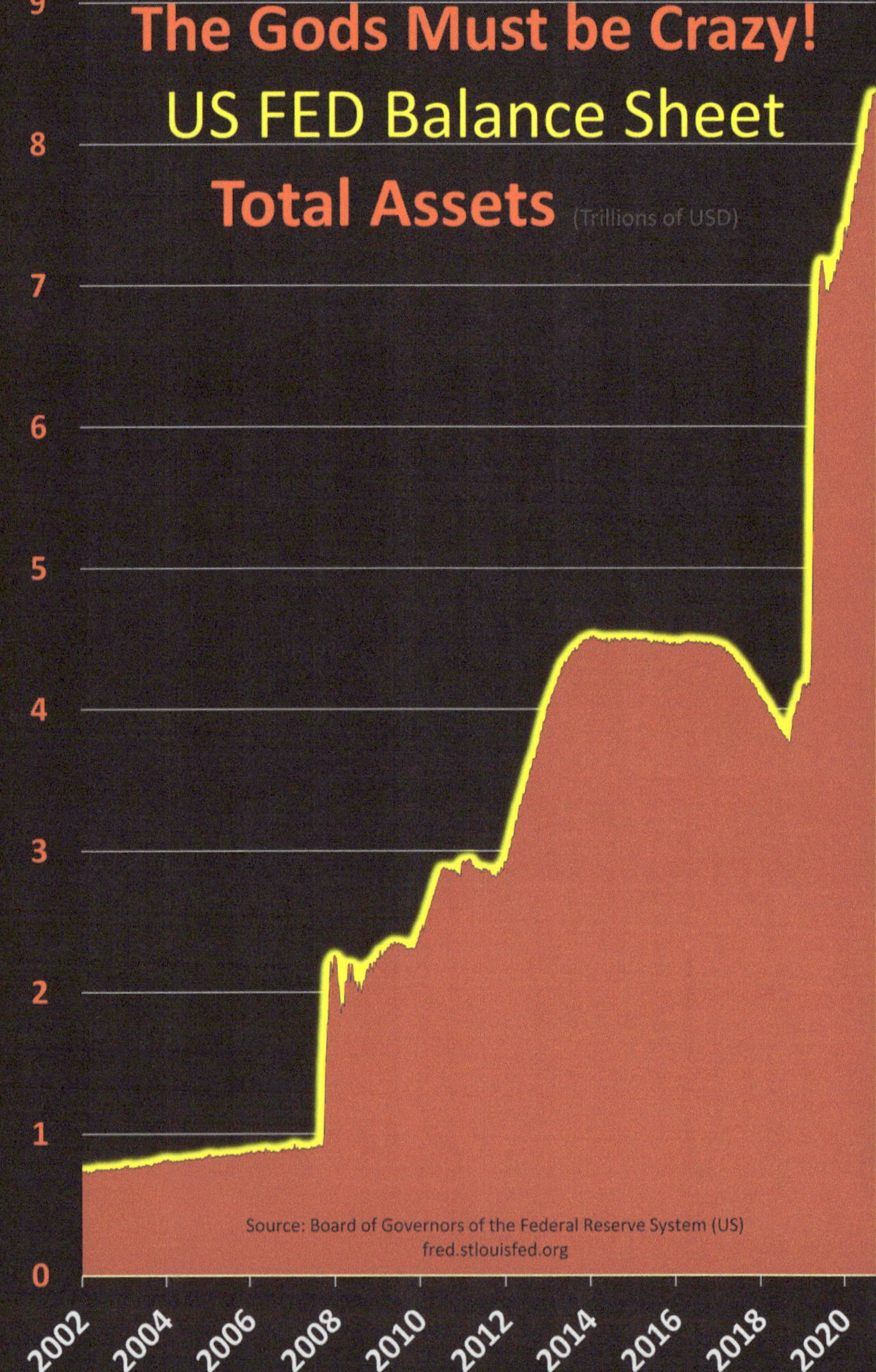
The Gods Must be Crazy!
US FED Balance Sheet
Total Assets (Trillions of USD)
Source: Board of Governors of the Federal Reserve System (US)
fred.stlouisfed.org
8
7
6
5
4
3
2
1
0
2002
2004
2006
2008
2010
2012
2014
2016
2018
2020

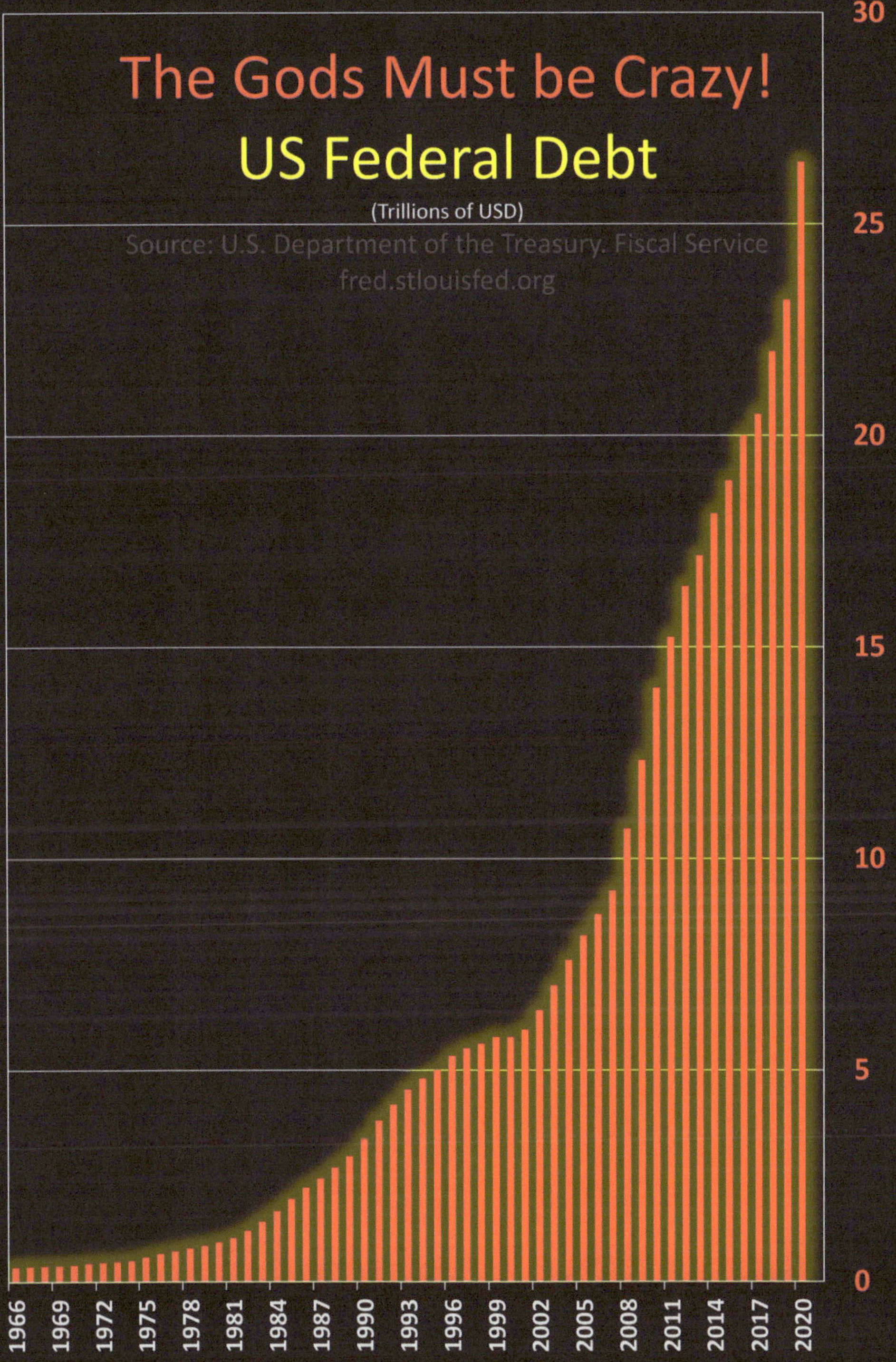
The Gods Must be Crazy!
US Federal Debt
(Trillions of USD)
Source: U.S. Department of the Treasury. Fiscal Service
fred.stlouisfed.org
30
25
20
15
10
5
0
1966
1969
1972
1975
1978
1981
1984
1987
1990
1993
1996
1999
2002
2005
2008
2011
2014
2017
2020

"We have to see that Chinese companies, partly with the support of state funds, are increasingly trying to buy up European companies that are cheap to acquire or that got into economic difficulties due to the coronavirus crisis...

China will be our biggest competitor in the future, in economic, social and political terms...

I view China as the strategic competitor for Europe, that represents an authoritarian model of society, that wants to expand its power and replace the United States as a leading power...

The European Union, therefore, should react in a coordinated way and put an end to the 'Chinese shopping tour.'"

Manfred Weber,

(Head of the EPP grouping in the EU Parliament (NPR News 5-17-20))

Once upon a different time, circa 1960, the US economy made up around 40% of the World's GDP. Alas, as we have seen, it has fallen to less than 15% in PPP. Meanwhile, China's GDP is roaring, with over 20% of the World's GDP currently. Our foolish extreme greed has squandered our goodwill. If we do not get our act together, and quickly, our Empire and Enterprise days are numbered – especially considering that we control 79.5% of all world trade thanks to our reserve currency status (the US dollar)[42].

The Planet of the Fourth Reich

In summary, many enterprises' state is akin to a group of dysfunctional Frankenstein zombies from the World War II era run by a top-down *good ole boys* club from the western ivory tower. As the world has evolved; today, most market growth occurs where 96% of 7.8 billion people live. The pundits from the ivory tower erred by looking only at the top of the pyramid. We need to re-architect business from a bottom-up perspective.

During the 1990s, George Soros broke the Bank of England for £3.3 billion[43] and caused the Asian Financial Crisis with only a fraction of his wealth[44]. According to Oxfam, Apple alone holds more than $200 billion in offshore funds, while the UK foreign exchange reserve is less than $180 billion. The United States holds less than $130 billion, while China sits on a honeypot with more than $3000 billion. As you can see from the graph, the US Federal Reserve balance sheet almost doubled in less than three months by adding a three trillion-dollar debt.

Sooner or later, the chickens will come home to roost. How many rogue dollars in the $25 trillion US debt (which includes the Chinese, Russian, and Saudi holdings) are needed to break the Western Capitalism Enterprise?

If we do not architect the 22nd Century digital age, "Noah's New Normal Enterprise Ark," we will soon be working as slaves for the *Man In The High Castle*[45], reminiscent of the Netflix Documentary *American Factory*[46]. Coronavirus may well become the trojan horse of the Fourth Reich.

THE CURRENT STATE OF ENTERPRISE

"Anger may in time change to gladness; vexation may be succeeded by content. But a kingdom that has once been destroyed can never come again into being; nor can the dead ever be brought back to life. Hence the enlightened ruler is heedful, and the good general full of caution. This is the way to keep a country at peace and an army intact."

Sun Tzu's The Art of War (476–221 BC)

In summary, the current state of Enterprises is a herd of dysfunctional patches of walking dead from the World War II era. They are decreed by a gang of top-down Good Old boys club from a western ivory tower. Unfortunately, the world has moved on, and today, as mentioned earlier, most of the market growth is where 96% of the 7.8 billion people live. We have a minimal stake and little understanding of the situation, which China is taking advantage of by economic and digital colonization. We need to re-architect the enterprise from the bottom-up perspective. The dear leaders from the halls of IVY erred by looking only at the top of the pyramid. As an example (based on my experience):

- So-called SNAKE OIL[47] salesmen build >75% of typical Enterprise Architectures today. Many are mostly a bunch of frogs in the well who architected on penny-wise, pound-foolish foundations. They are rotten with political egos in finance/business, IT, implementation partners, offshore vendors, Big 4 PPTs, ...
- The bigger the fortune (company size), the less desirable the enterprise
- >75% of typical enterprise implementations are *screwed.*
- >75% of typical enterprise survivors are dysfunctional Frankenstein zombies from M&A, reverse mergers, inversion, TESCM, BPO, transformations, layoffs, outsourcing, and other modes of excessive financial engineering.
- >75% of architecture for typical enterprises predates the World Wide Web (WWW) era – in other words, this architecture does not correspond with the Digital Age. IT, traditional accounting, and most business functions (especially repetitive) are on the verge of automation by AI BOTs in the cloud. IT/Business systems will evolve from Transactional -> Operational –> Predictive Analytics AI BOTs (Robotic Automation in Cloud).

"Alice: Would you tell me, please, which way I ought to go from here?
CAT: THAT DEPENDS A GOOD DEAL ON WHERE YOU WANT TO GET TO.
Alice: I don't much care where.
CAT: THEN IT DOESN'T MUCH MATTER WHICH WAY YOU GO"
– Alice in Wonderland

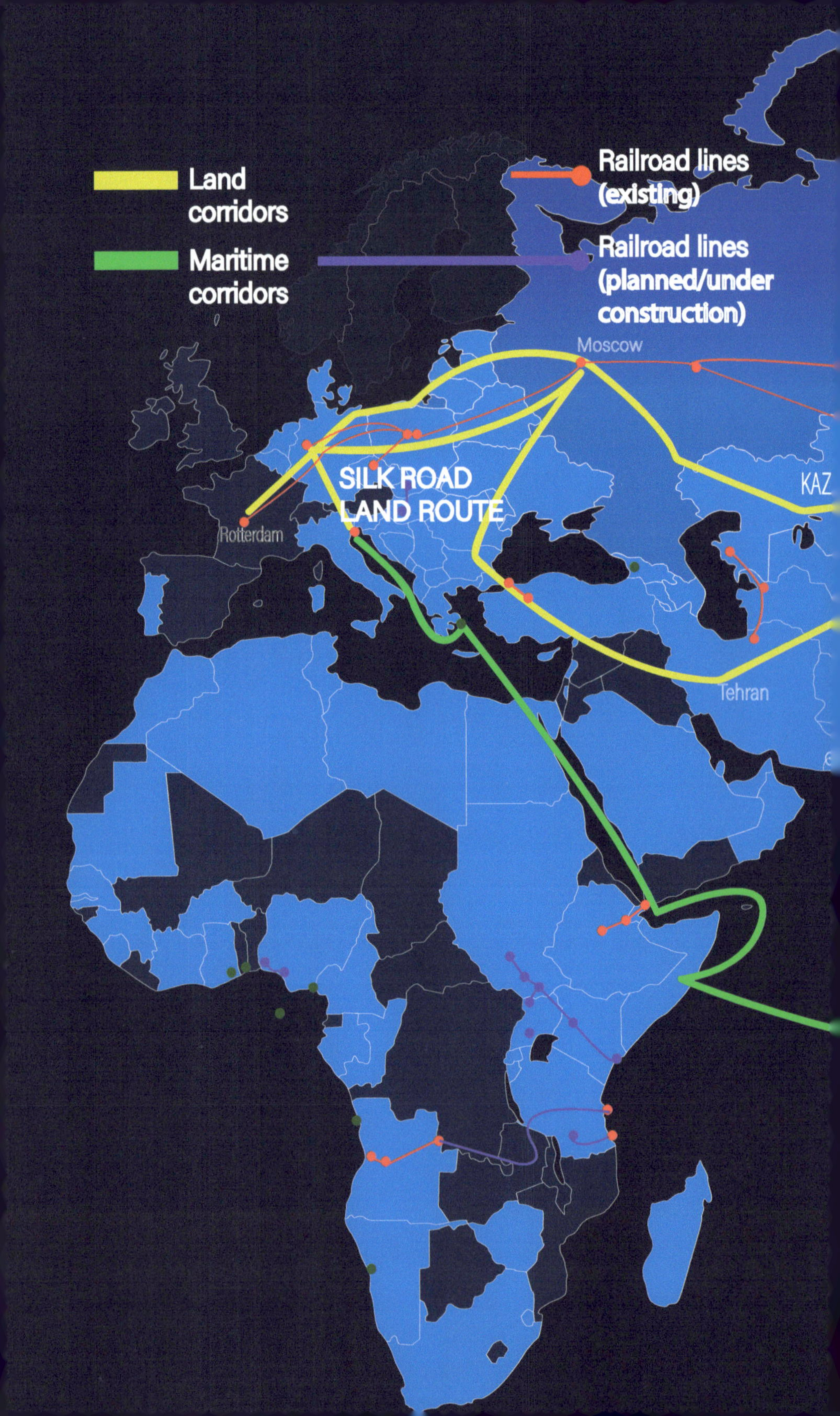

Land corridors
Maritime corridors
Railroad lines (existing)
Railroad lines (planned/under construction)
Moscow
KAZ
SILK ROAD LAND ROUTE
Rotterdam
Tehran

Ports with Chinese engagement (existing)
Ports with Chinese engagement (planned/ under construction)
RUSSIA
XINJIANG REGION
Mongolia
Xian
CHINA
Kolkata
MYANMAR
Kuala Lumpur
SILK ROAD SEA ROUTE
As of 2013,82% of China's oil imports and 20% of its gas imports pass through the Strait of Malacca

China spends trillions of dollars propping up its quasi enterprises and has already vastly surpassed its 2025 targets set by the CCP (Communist Party of China) in 2015. They have already mercilessly eliminated their western competitors on higher-value products and services such as 5G, technology infrastructure, aerospace, and semiconductors. They have achieved independence from foreign suppliers for such products and services.

Now, western enterprise's pre-WWW (World Wide Web) architecture is abused and outdated. It has lost its resiliency and cannot compete with enterprises from the east. Today, we face these challenges because of the corrupt system in Washington DC, Gordon Gekko's Private Equity and corporate raiders (some funded by Chinese), Twitter-driven Wall Street algorithms, and the resulting excessive financial manipulation.

Our leaders became disconnected from reality. Dwelling in their pristine temples of rigged capitalism, they cook up financial schemes. In the past ten years, the stock market shot up over 250% without any productive growth, and financial engineering abused the excellent balance sheet. They have been shaking the very foundations of capitalism.

"In a material economic slowdown scenario, half as severe as the global financial crisis, corporate debt-at-risk (debt owed by firms that are unable to cover their interest expenses with their earnings) could rise to $19 trillion—or nearly 40 percent of total corporate debt in major economies—above crisis levels."

— Global Financial Stability Report, IMF (2019)[48]

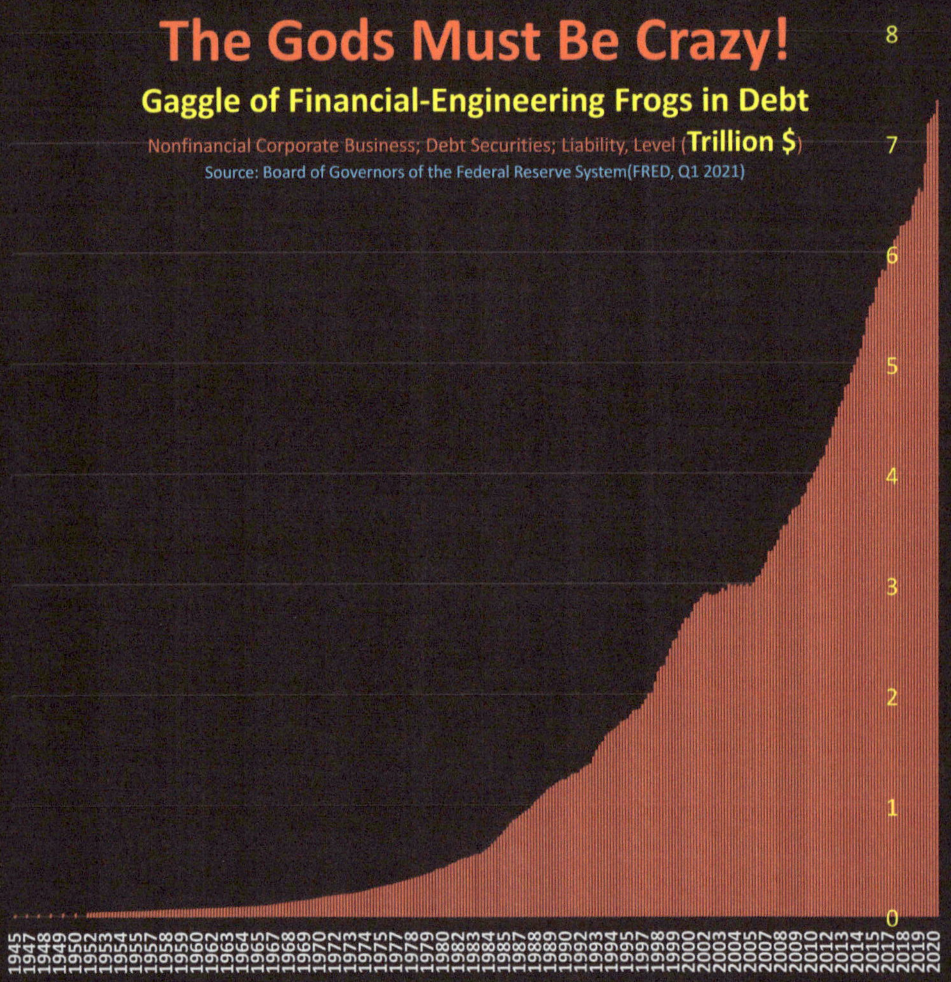

★★★★★★★★★★★★★★★★★★★★★★★★★

Many of today's large enterprises are mainly walking dead conglomerations from M&A, Reverse Mergers, Inversion, TESCM, BPO, Transformations, Layoffs, Outsourcing, and other modes of excessive financial engineering. The bulk of these enterprises will seal their own fate at the hands of Chinese intellectual property (IP) vultures, as in the chart below:

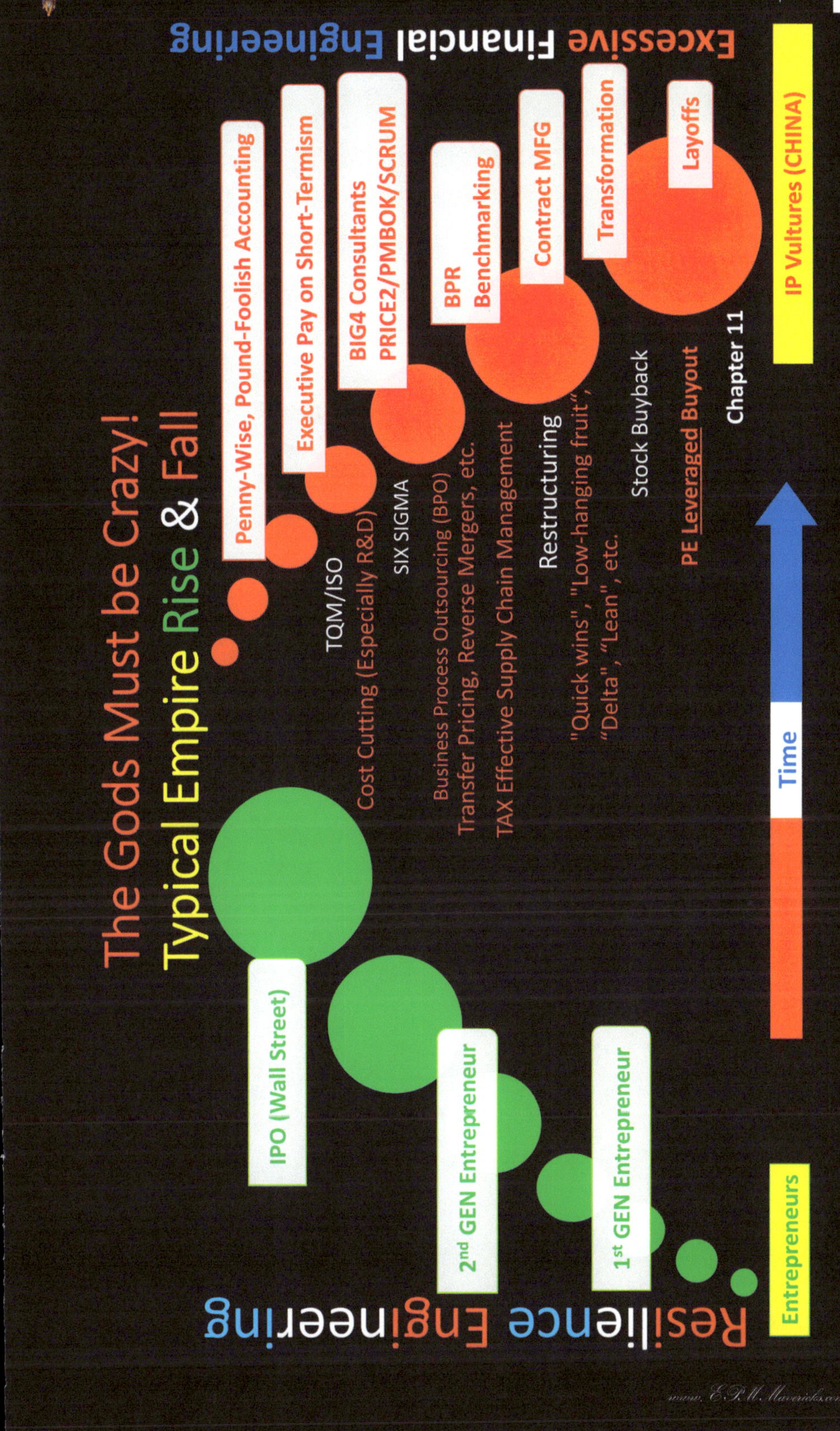
The Gods Must be Crazy!
Typical Empire Rise & Fall
Resilience Engineering
Excessive Financial Engineering
Entrepreneurs
1st GEN Entrepreneur
2nd GEN Entrepreneur
IPO (Wall Street)
TQM/ISO
Cost Cutting (Especially R&D)
SIX SIGMA
Business Process Outsourcing (BPO)
Transfer Pricing, Reverse Mergers, etc.
TAX Effective Supply Chain Management
Restructuring
"Quick wins", "Low-hanging fruit",
"Delta", "Lean", etc.
Stock Buyback
PE Leveraged Buyout
Chapter 11
Penny-Wise, Pound-Foolish Accounting
Executive Pay on Short-Termism
BIG4 Consultants
PRICE2/PMBOK/SCRUM
BPR
Benchmarking
Contract MFG
Transformation
Layoffs
Time
IP Vultures (CHINA)

"We have to see that Chinese companies, partly with the support of state funds, are increasingly trying to buy up European companies that are cheap to acquire or that got into economic difficulties due to the coronavirus crisis...China will be our biggest competitor in the future, in economic, social, and political terms...

I view China as the strategic competitor for Europe, that represents an authoritarian model of society, that wants to expand its power and replace the United States as a leading power...

The European Union, therefore, should react in a coordinated way and put an end to the "Chinese shopping tour."

Manfred Weber

(Head of the EPP grouping in the EU Parliament (NPR News 5-17-20))

Ay Yi Yai Yi! We are in the middle of The New World Order!

THE GODS MUST BE CRAZY![49]

MY JOURNEY FROM THE LAND OF COMMUNISTS TO THE EPITOME OF CAPITALISM

"Knowing the enemy enables you to take the offensive, knowing yourself enables you to stand on the defensive." He adds: "Attack is the secret of defense; defense is the planning of an attack."

Sun Tzu's The Art of War (476–221 BC)

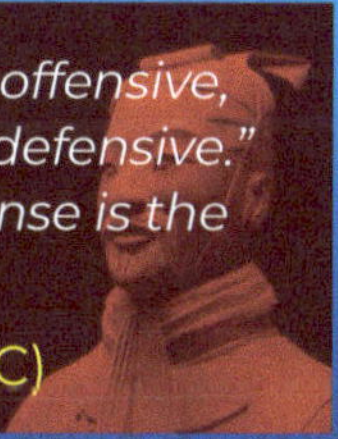

Let me confess; I am a prodigal capitalistic cowboy son of socialist parents from God's own country, Kerala, India. Thanks to Catholic schools, run by the missionaries brought by our European colonizers, communists have been democratically elected for more than half a century in Kerala, with Marx, Lenin, Stalin, and Che being worshipped by our people as super-gods. Though we belong to the middle class, my parents, who were both teachers, never had the luxury of taking vacations back then, so I spent most school holidays at Dad's college library reading western travelogues.

We did not have a TV at home, and the only movie they ever took me to the theater to see was *Gandhi*. Ironically, I eventually became the global EPM architect at the #1 showbusiness in the world, AMC Theatres, owned by one-time China's richest man. As a result of my liberation, or perhaps as an act of vengeance for the past two decades, I squandered the money my hardworking wife earned by chasing birds and brandishing my camera in the global wildernesses across 20 countries. Thanks to the Chinese *GIFT executive leadership program*[50] (https://global-inst.com/learn/) in Cambodia's killing fields[51], I found solace by trekking the jungles of Chiangmai-Chiangrai, Laos, and Myanmar in search of snake wine[52]. While sipping the snake wine, I would wonder, how come these resource-rich countries are so impoverished? (According to Hernando de Soto's research, such countries have more wealth than the 12 main western stock markets combined.) Yet, these countries are economically colonized by China and are begging Western charities who try to greenwash their guilt.

In the "New Normal" age, where the world is losing confidence in an unregulated government currency printing press on Helicopter (quantitative easing (QE)[53]), ironically, a useless yellow metal (gold) is again becoming the *gold* standard for the wealth of nations and the filthy rich. For more than a century, the US sucked up most of the world's declared gold reserve, about 8,000 metric tons. Behind them, the old European guards together holding another 10,000 tons. Believe it or not, as per the World Gold Council (WGC), the poorest of the poor Indian women are illegally hiding more than 25,000 tons of that same useless yellow metal under their mattresses (an underground economy). In search of answers to *The Mystery of Capital*, I became the voodoo worshipper of Hernando de Soto and his book *The Mystery of Capital: Why Capitalism Triumphs in the West and Fails Everywhere Else*.

Let me share some of my personal experiences on this mystery. It took my parents nearly three decades to build their home after saving 97% of the construction cost. It took them another decade to repay the remaining 3% at an interest rate of 30% from loan sharks. Being a prodigal cowboy capitalist, I've hardly saved any money to date. To be frank, I've had little faith in that meaningless piece of paper that says, *In God We Trust*.

"The hour of capitalism's greatest triumph is its hour of crisis."

Hernando de Soto
(*The Mystery of Capital: Why Capitalism Triumphs in the West and Fails Everywhere Else*)

While everyone was deleveraging during the 2008 economic Tsunami, I became a quintessence Gordon Gekko seeking to leverage capitalism. I managed to snap up two iconic properties in North America (valued at over a million dollars), in rapid succession (within two years). I took a 97% mortgage loan, and within a few months, I'd refinanced it and cashed out over 1000% of the down payment for a sweet 30-year loan at a ~3% interest rate.

"The hour of capitalism's greatest triumph is its hour of crisis."

Hernando de Soto

(*The Mystery of Capital: Why Capitalism Triumphs in the West and Fails Everywhere Else*)

Against conventional wisdom, I also calculated bets on international markets and the muddy waters of currency, which paid off exponentially. I visited China a couple of times as well (in addition to my Chinese *GIFT executive leadership program* (https://global-inst.com/learn/), I used to be responsible for PMI China as PMI Asian Regional Mentor too). I capitalized on the explosive Extreme Financial Engineering market and reincarnated to an EPM career out of the 2008 economic tsunami, ending up in the BIG4 world. The more I looked at the finance world in the West, the more disillusioned I became.

The Financial Engineering termites have infested the western capitalist mainframe built by Roosevelt. Now, it is collapsing like a house of cards. Communist authoritarianism (EAST) is economically colonizing the world through debt-trap diplomacy. After two decades, it looks like I'll need to ride back through that Mad Max fury road and climb through the capitalist rubble from Roosevelt's legacy.

Ay Yi Yai Yi! We are in the middle of The New World Order!

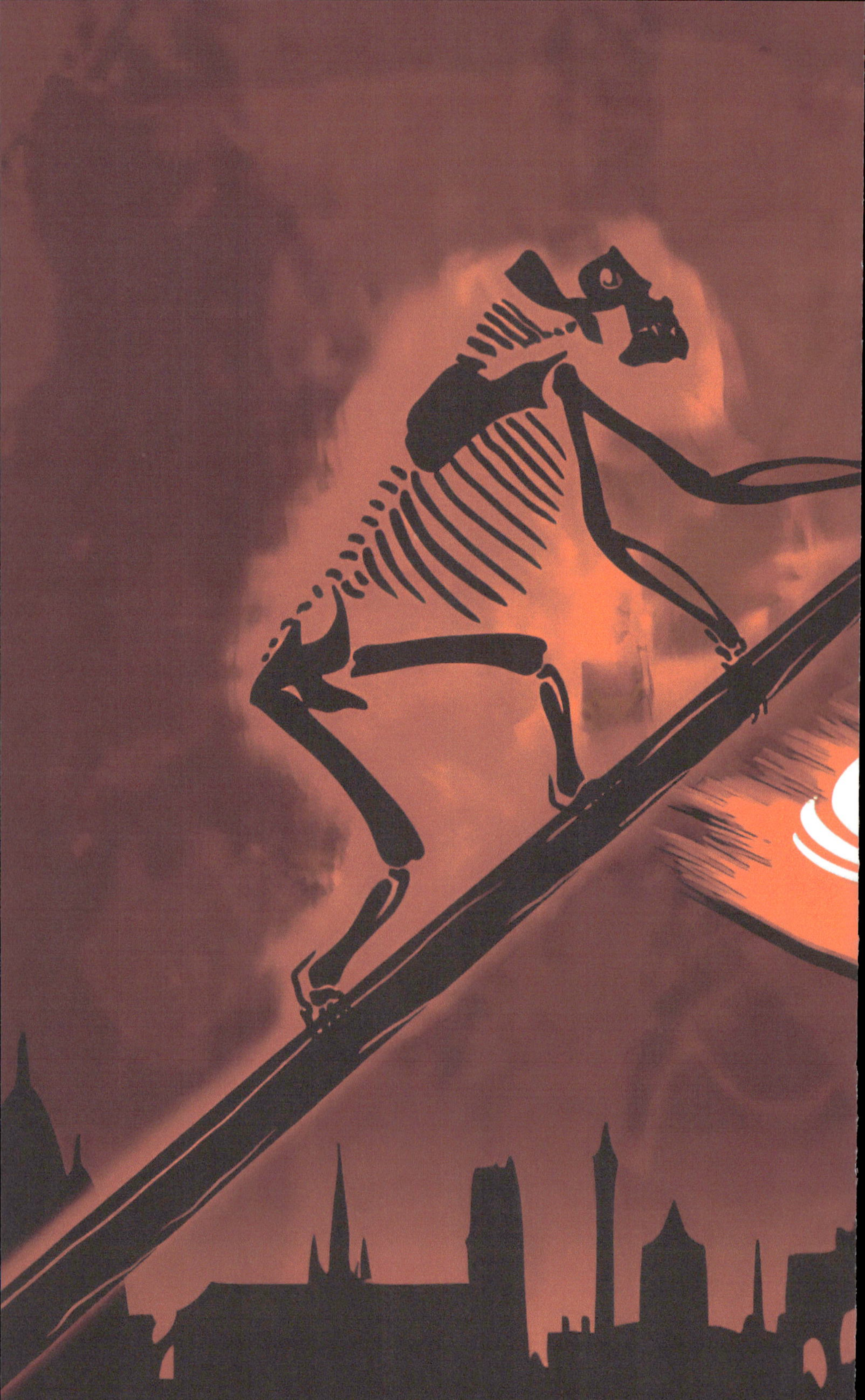

THE NEW WORLD ORDER

"All warfare is based on deception. Hence, when able to attack, we must seem unable; when using our forces, we must seem inactive; when we are near, we must make the enemy believe we are far away; when far away, we must make him believe we are near."

Sun Tzu's The Art of War (476–221 BC)

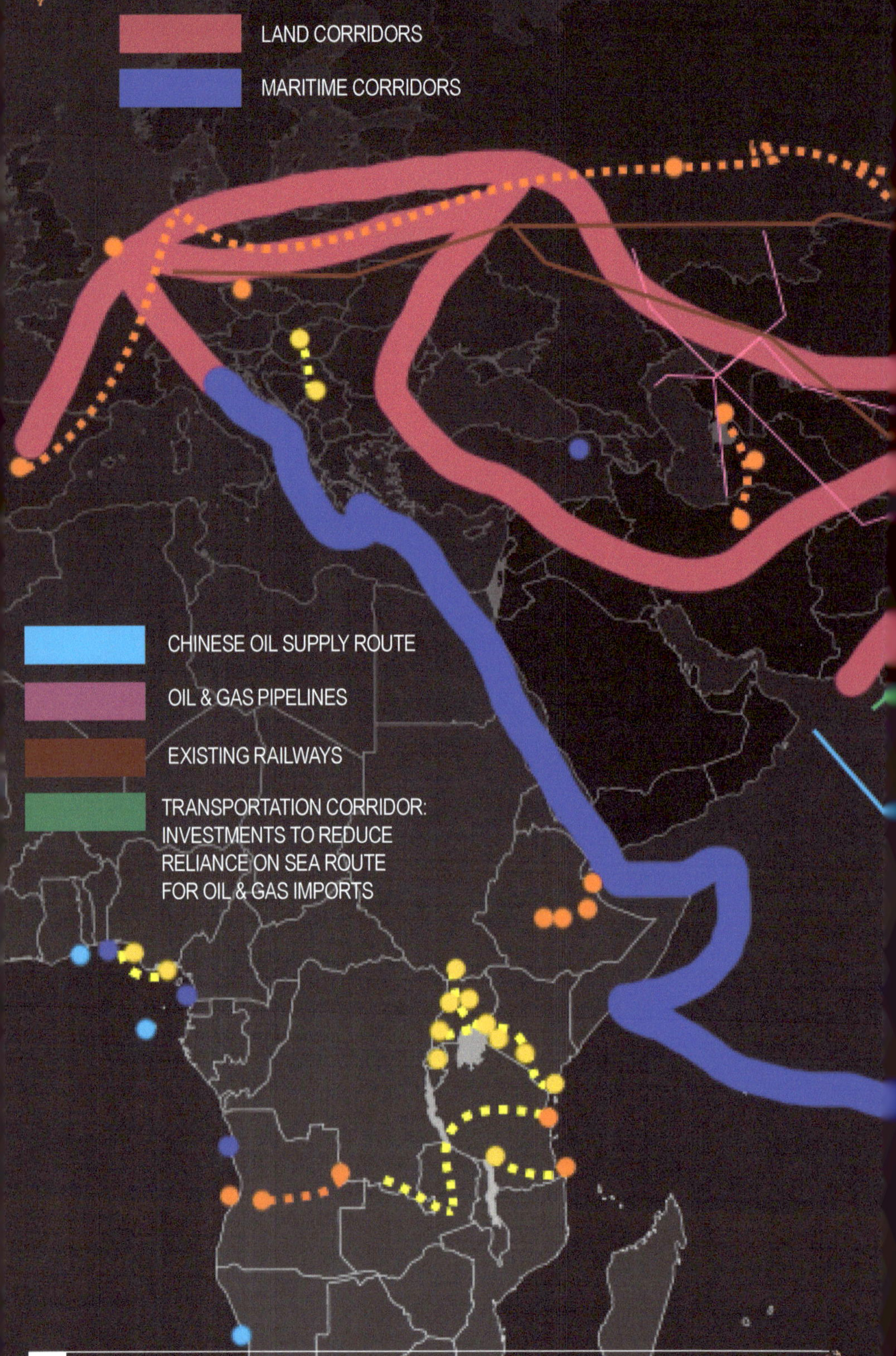
LAND CORRIDORS
MARITIME CORRIDORS
CHINESE OIL SUPPLY ROUTE
OIL & GAS PIPELINES
EXISTING RAILWAYS
TRANSPORTATION CORRIDOR: INVESTMENTS TO REDUCE RELIANCE ON SEA ROUTE FOR OIL & GAS IMPORTS

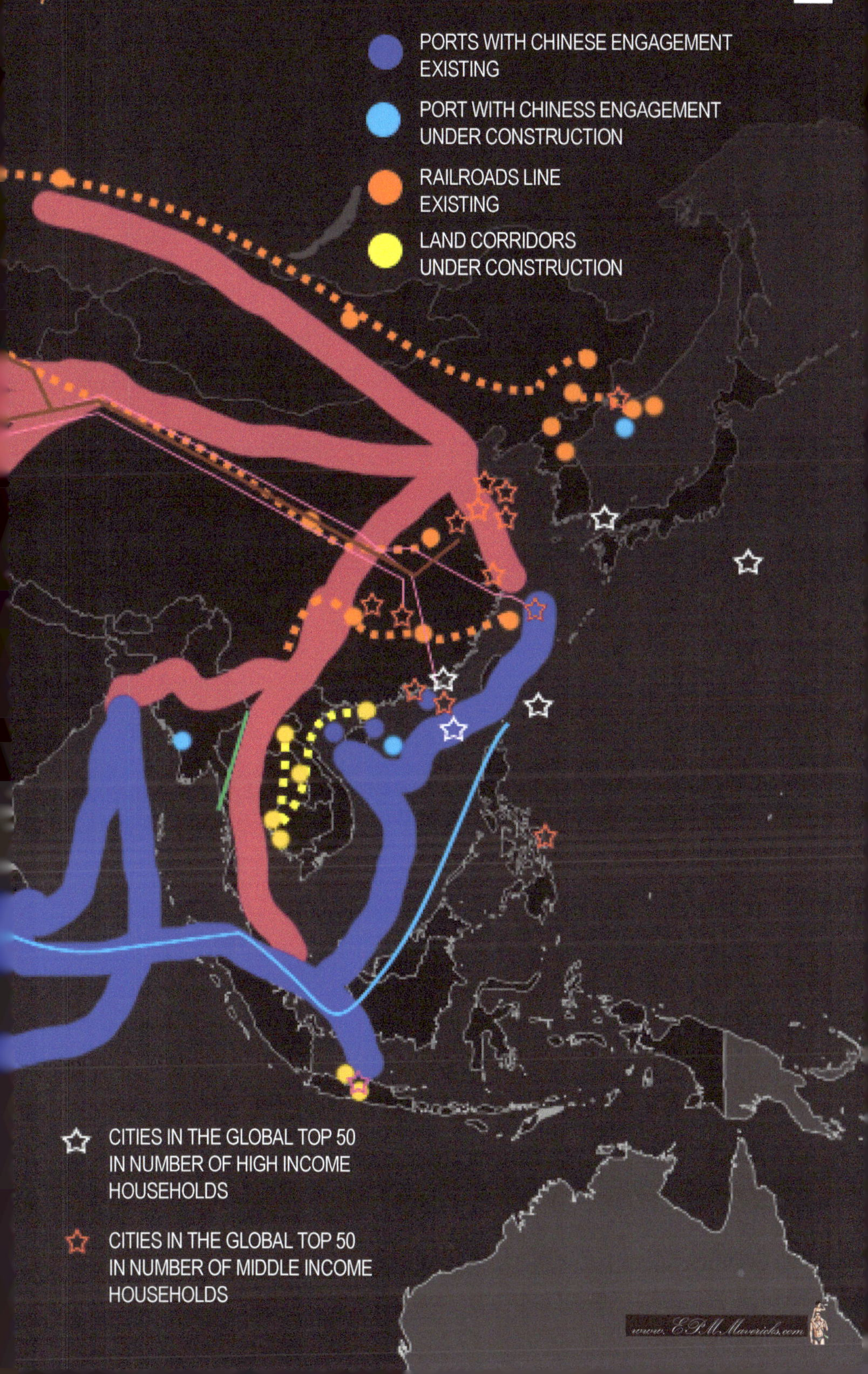
PORTS WITH CHINESE ENGAGEMENT EXISTING
PORT WITH CHINESS ENGAGEMENT UNDER CONSTRUCTION
RAILROADS LINE EXISTING
LAND CORRIDORS UNDER CONSTRUCTION
CITIES IN THE GLOBAL TOP 50 IN NUMBER OF HIGH INCOME HOUSEHOLDS
CITIES IN THE GLOBAL TOP 50 IN NUMBER OF MIDDLE INCOME HOUSEHOLDS

While hunkering down due to COVID, I had the opportunity to analyze how I found myself in the epitome of capitalism. Thanks to the Roosevelts, we, the US, became an exceptional empire on the globe a century ago. Unfortunately, it appears the cheese has now moved back from whence I came (the East).

I have an understanding of how and when Empires rise and fall. For example, the most prominent enterprises to date are the 17th century Dutch East India Company (~$10 trillion) and the 18th century British East India Company (~$5 trillion), all via whipping (colonization) and stealing dollars from my forefathers. Those enterprises and empires lasted for around 200 years each.

The thought-provoking story of their rise and fall piqued my curiosity. How do their tales compare to the enterprises of the current state of empires? It became clear that the next authoritarian Emperor is banging on our door to once again economically (and digitally) colonize us, much like what happened to my grandfathers. In the post-COVID era, where China is on an extremely accelerated course, I fear that we are doomed to fall like a knife. With an eye to the bloody history, I cannot help but wonder what kind of 'New Normal' lies ahead of us.

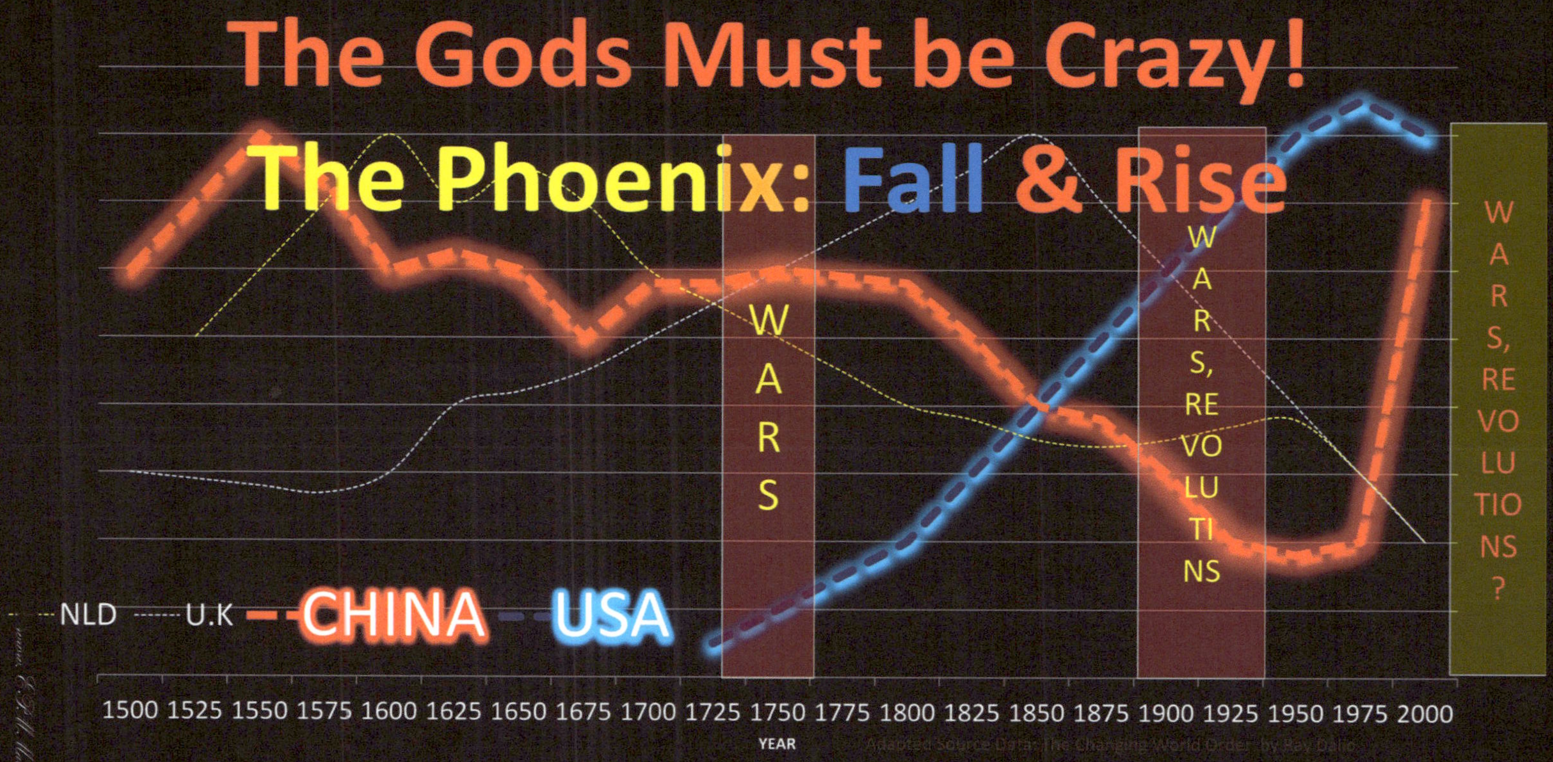
The Gods Must be Crazy!
The Phoenix: Fall & Rise
NLD
U.K
CHINA
USA
WARS
WARS, REVOLUTINS
WARS, REVOLUTIONS ?
1500 1525 1550 1575 1600 1625 1650 1675 1700 1725 1750 1775 1800 1825 1850 1875 1900 1925 1950 1975 2000
YEAR
Adapted Source Data: The Changing World Order by Ray Dalio

Ay Yi Yai Yi! We are in the middle of The New World Order!

Ay Yi Yai Yi! We are in the middle of The New World Order!

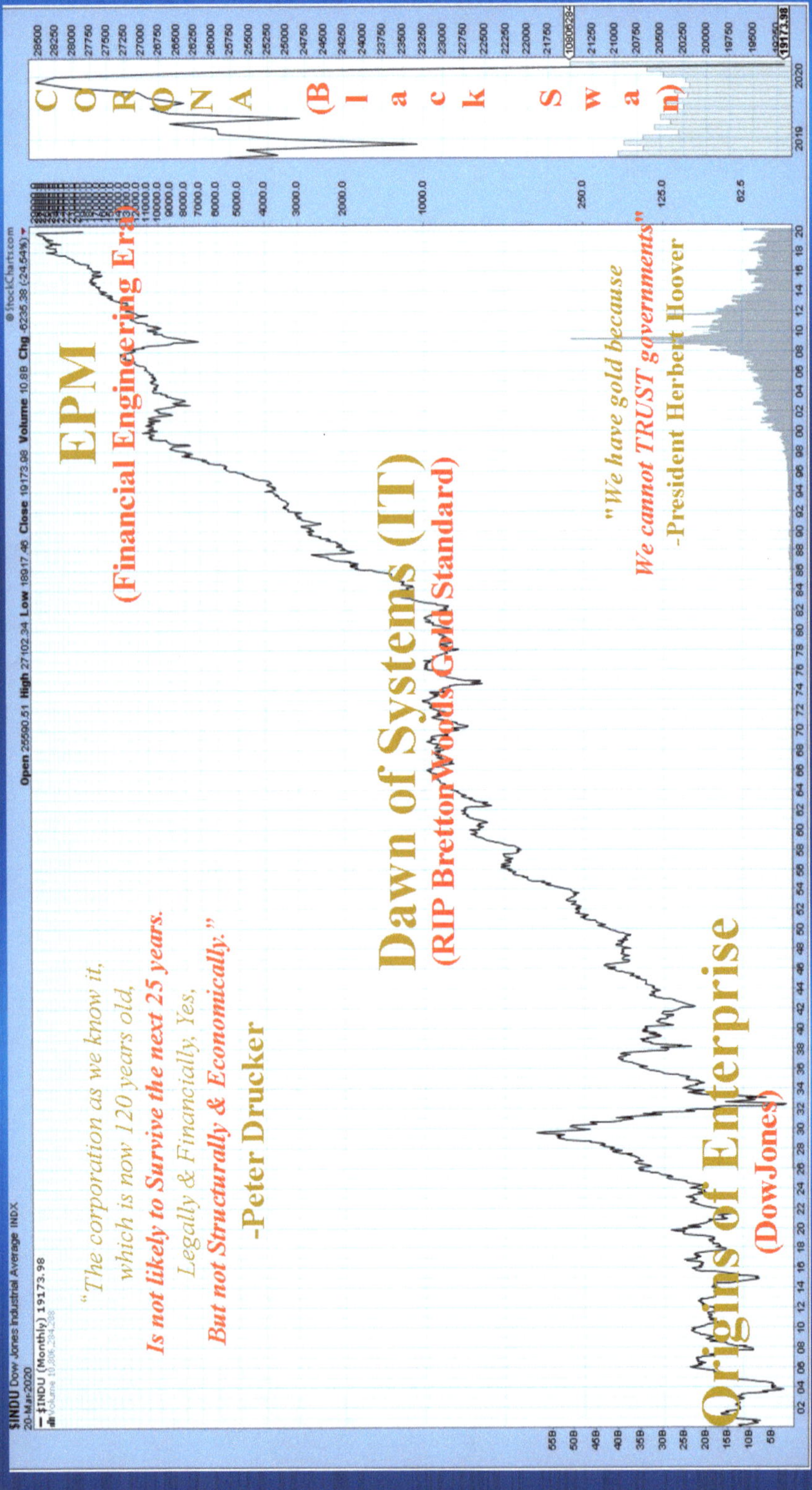
$INDU Dow Jones Industrial Average INDX
20-Mar-2020
Open 25590.51 High 27102.34 Low 18917.46 Close 19173.98 Volume 10.8B Chg -6235.38 (-24.54%)
©StockCharts.com
"The corporation as we know it, which is now 120 years old, Is not likely to Survive the next 25 years. Legally & Financially, Yes, But not Structurally & Economically."
-Peter Drucker
Origins of Enterprise
(DowJones)
Dawn of Systems (IT)
(RIP Bretton Woods Gold Standard)
EPM
(Financial Engineering Era)
"We have gold because We cannot TRUST governments"
-President Herbert Hoover
CORONA
(Black Swan)

THE NEW ENTERPRISE ORDER

I will test my hypothesis using the prediction of my beloved MBA management guru two-and-a-half decades ago:

"The corporation as we know it, which is now 120 years old, It is not likely to survive the next 25 years. Legally and Financially, yes, But not Structurally and Economically."

Peter Drucker, Circa 2000

"Every kingdom divided against itself is laid to waste, and no city or house divided against itself will stand"

Sun Tzu's The Art of War (476–221 BC)

My hypothesis, which I've developed since the last economic tsunami hinging on the Dow Jones index, is illustrated below:

Central Tenets of the Hypothesis

The survival of the enterprise is umbilically dependent on the success of the ecosystems around it. The ecosystem undoubtedly depends on its sponsoring godfather Empire.

I believe that the godfather Empire's survival depends on particular measures of strength, which are:

1. Leadership
2. STEM (Science, Technology, Engineering, and Mathematics) Education
3. Research and Strategic Technology
4. Infrastructure Architecture
5. Digital Architecture
6. Knowledge Management
7. Diplomacy
8. World Currency Gold Standard
9. Electro-Dollar
10. Financial Capital
11. Security
12. Transformative Digital Grand Strategies and Regulations

The picture below depicts how the Rise and Fall of various godfathering Empires have transpired in the past four centuries.

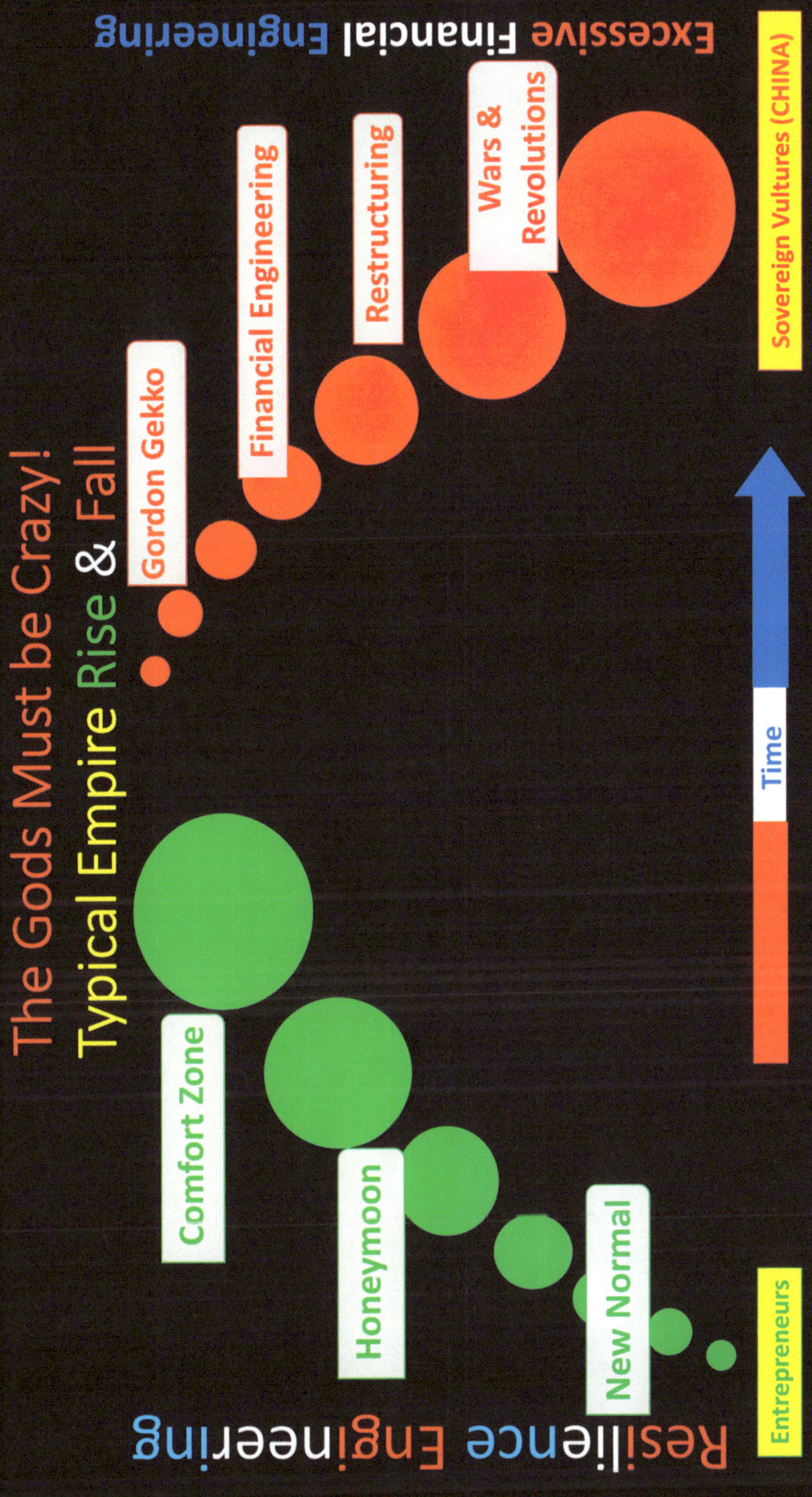
The Gods Must be Crazy!
Typical Empire Rise & Fall
Resilience Engineering
Excessive Financial Engineering
Entrepreneurs
New Normal
Honeymoon
Comfort Zone
Gordon Gekko
Financial Engineering
Restructuring
Wars & Revolutions
Sovereign Vultures (CHINA)
Time

Ay Yi Yai Yi! We are in the middle of The New World Order!

"Consider your origin. You were not formed to live like brutes but to follow virtue and knowledge."

Dante Alighieri

Ay Yi Yai Yi! We are in the middle of The New World Order!

At the beginning of an empire, there is a honeymoon period of tribal harmony and prosperity. But when that empire falls into its comfort zone, it becomes overconfident and its lifestyle changes. As its lifestyle changes, it becomes greedy. Greed is the foundation of capitalism, which leads to a Gordon Gekko[54] (the icon for extreme greed in the classic Oscar-winning movie "Wall Street") period of leveraged capitalism. This thrill of the bubble ride leads to higher and higher levels of testosterone. One day, the bubble bursts, and we start distorting reality (financial engineering). Distorting reality will take us to more significant tectonic shifts, and then we will start cooking the books through quantitative easing[55]. Finally, when the economic tsunami hits, there will be wars and revolutions. All the scavengers will come together and decide on the new tribal order; this is currently happening to us.

Unfortunately, **it's halftime, America, and our second half is about to begin!**[56]

I sincerely hope that if we in the WEST play our trump cards right, **we can excel in our second half too**.

"Consider your origin. You were not formed to live like brutes but to follow virtue and knowledge."

Dante Alighieri

We have a formidable dragon that has been shaking his champagne bottle for the past two decades and is impatiently waiting to pop the cork in the post-COVID era. The Chinese dragon is on an upward trajectory, and we are falling fast, which only increases the threat. I sincerely believe we can at least smooth the curve of decline and avoid the catastrophic transformations if we play our cards right.

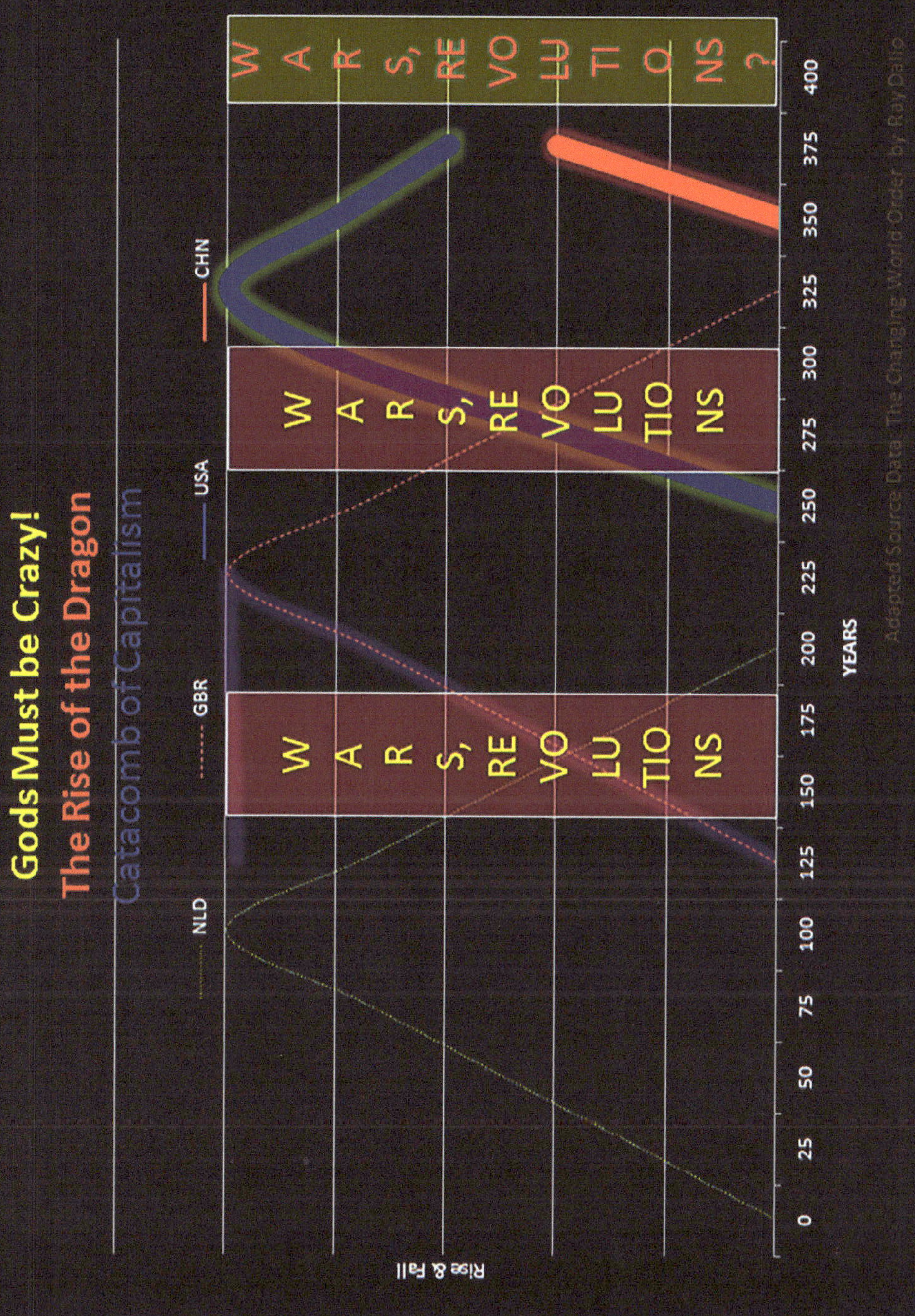
Gods Must be Crazy!
The Rise of the Dragon
Catacomb of Capitalism
NLD
GBR
USA
CHN
Rise & Fall
WARS, REVOLUTIONS
WARS, REVOLUTIONS
WARS, REVOLUTIONS?
0
25
50
75
100
125
150
175
200
225
250
275
300
325
350
375
400
YEARS
Adapted Source Data: The Changing World Order by Ray Dalio

Ay Yi Yai Yi! We are in the middle of The New World Order!

Ay Yi Yai Yi! We are in the middle of The New World Order!

Si Vis Pacem, Para Bellum
If you want Enterprise peace,
prepare for EPM Architectural war

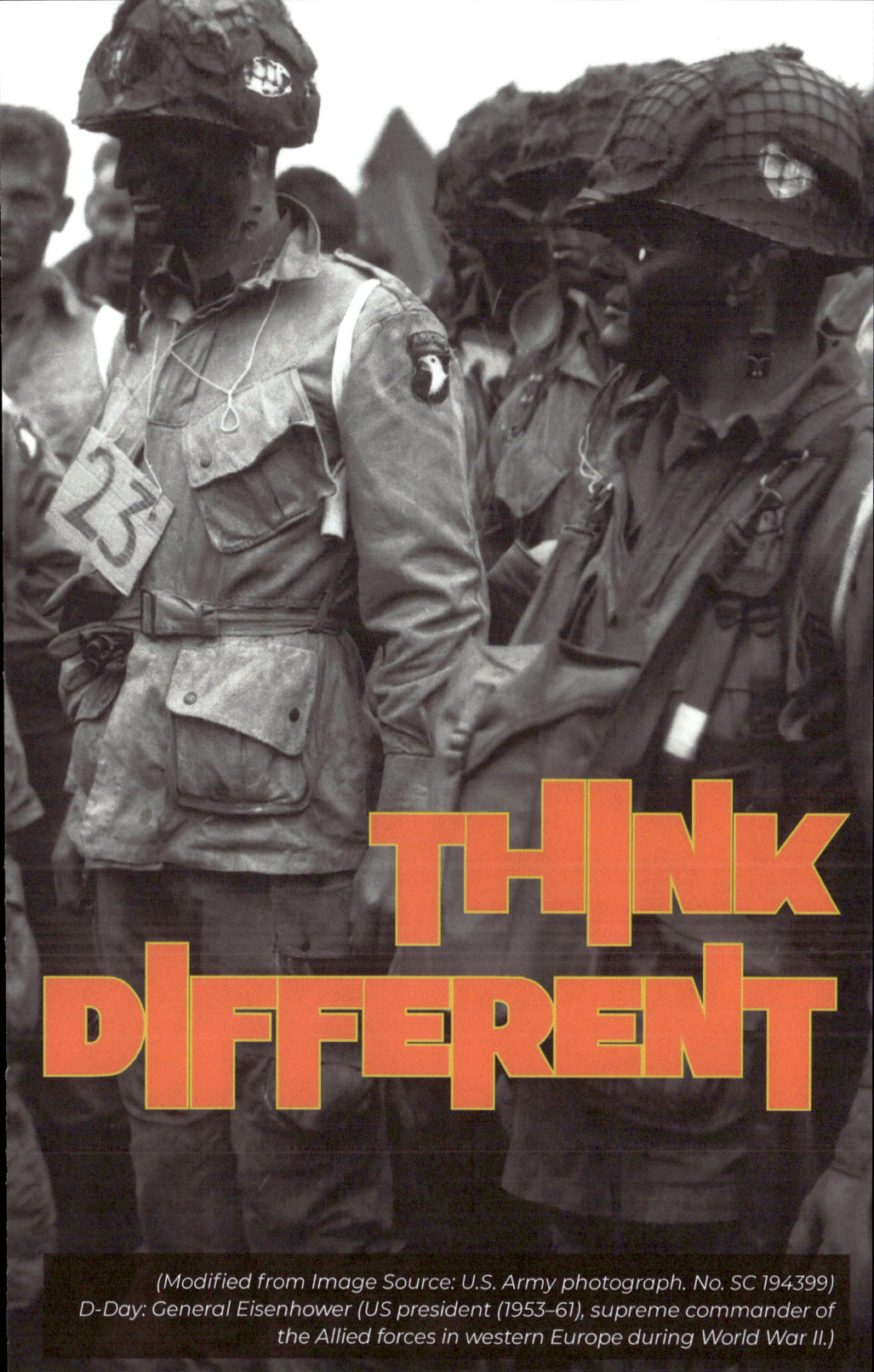

(Modified from Image Source: U.S. Army photograph. No. SC 194399)
D-Day: General Eisenhower (US president (1953–61), supreme commander of the Allied forces in western Europe during World War II.)

"MARTIN: Beijing is being very high profile about the aid that it's delivering to countries hard hit by the coronavirus. Do you worry that China has started to use soft power in a way that will further undermine America's influence on the global stage?

GATES: Yes. And they intend to do more. And what's worse, we have - as the book points out, we have weakened all of the instruments of power other than our military. And the reality is if we're lucky and we're smart, we won't have a military conflict with China. But the conflict will take place, the rivalry will take place, in all these other arenas, and that's where we are unprepared. And we have no strategy."

Former US Defense Secretary Robert Gates (NPR)

Ay Yi Yai Yi! We are in the middle of The New World Order!

Composite of Eleanor Roosevelt, Franklin D. Roosevelt, and Teddy Roosevelt (Courtesy, Franklin D. Roosevelt Presidential Library and Theodore Roosevelt Collection, Houghton Library, Harvard University)

WHO BUILT THE US CAPITALISTIC EMPIRE?

It would behoove us at this point to look at the origins of the American Empire. American Presidents hold the most formidable office in the world and triumph in a unique place at the epicenter of national and world events. I analyzed all our presidents since 1900 to discover the origins of our empire. Who were the emperors of those good old days, and what were their guiding principles?

"Never doubt that a small group of thoughtful, committed citizens can change the world. Indeed, it's the only thing that ever has."

Margaret Mead

"Victorious warriors win first and then go to war, while defeated warriors go to war first and then seek to win."

Sun Tzu's The Art of War (476–221 BC)

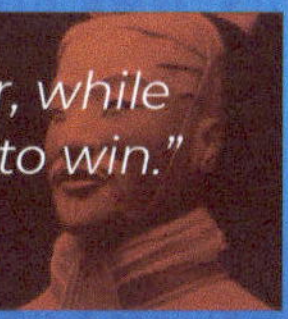

I found the answers had already been discovered a century ago. The great American Capitalistic Empire was architected by Roosevelt in the first half of the 20th century. As commander-in-chief, Presidents are irrefutably the most significant architects in world history. Despicably, it has been systematically dismantled and undone through Amerixit (an American version of self-proclaimed Talaq[57] (divorce in Islam) from global superpower status – similar to the UK's Brexit from EU). The US needs to revert to the 'Dust Bowl' from which Roosevelt once rescued capitalism. Roosevelts masterminded the framework for past semi-sesquicentennial peace and prosperity of the world through ending World War II. They also laid the foundations for the UN, WHO, UNESCO, UNICEF, Human Rights, and more. Instead of dismantling those institutions and taking us into the Fourth Reich, we need to strive to improve them and make them more robust.

The US Economy, which Roosevelt built, was around 40% (in 1960) of the World's GDP. It is now less than 15% in PPP and sinking fast. Meanwhile, China is over 20%[58] and is at full throttle. It is time to learn from the original architects of US capitalism. We must prepare for the imminent war so we might rebuild it before it is too late.

We need to *pray* to bring back the Good Old "New Deal" and genuine leaders like the Roosevelts (Theodore, FDR, and Eleanor). They faced similar strife during challenging historical moments a century ago, such as WWI, the Spanish Flu, the Great Depression, and WWII. We must search for our fading trump cards in the original dust bowl of the Roosevelts.

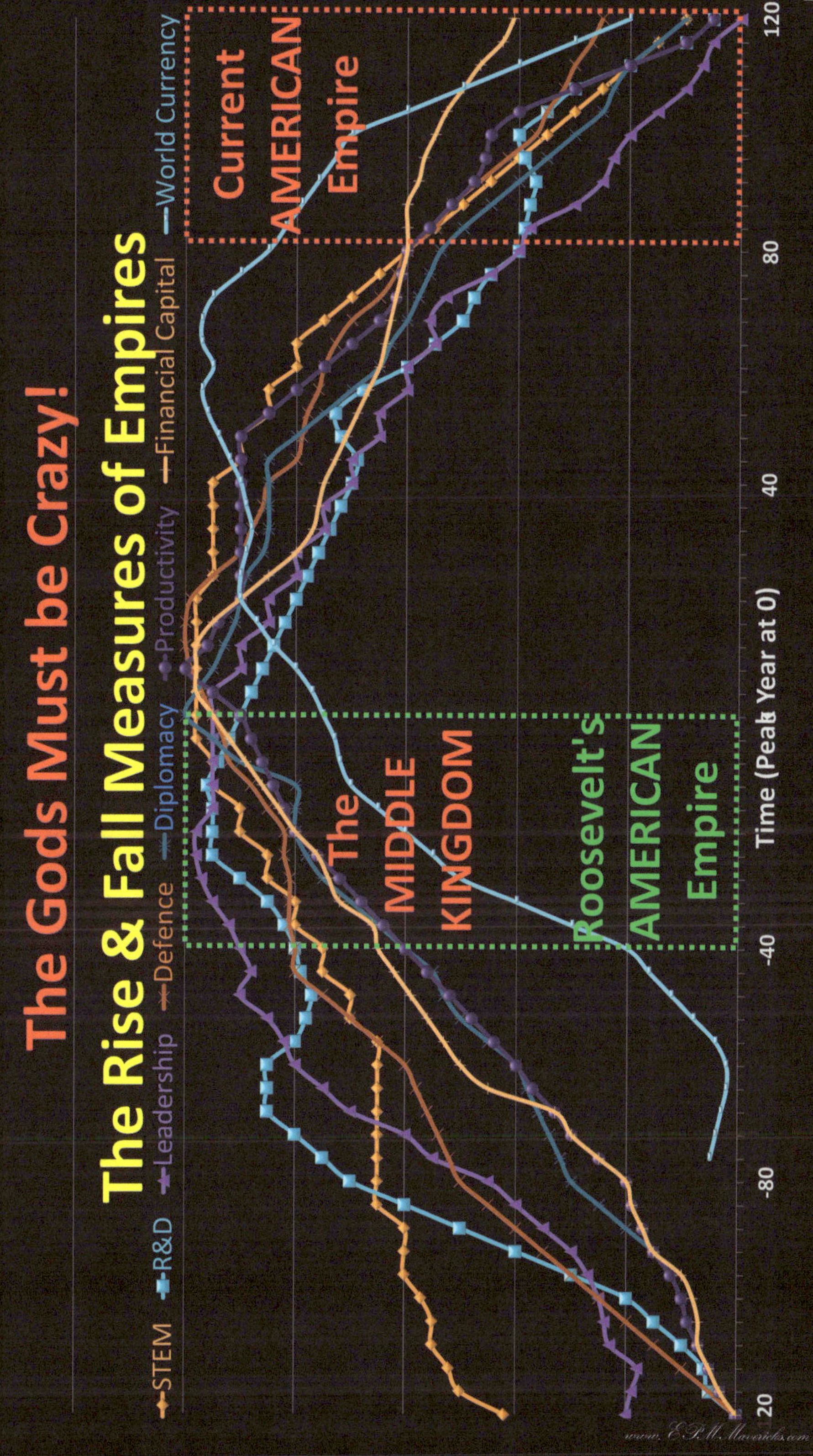
The Gods Must be Crazy!
The Rise & Fall Measures of Empires
STEM
R&D
Leadership
Defence
Diplomacy
Productivity
Financial Capital
World Currency
Current AMERICAN Empire
The MIDDLE KINGDOM
Roosevelt's AMERICAN Empire
20
-80
-40
40
80
120
Time (Peak Year at 0)
www.E.P.M.Mavericks.com

Those cards were the *measures of strength:*

(The following list are those measures, but they have adapted to today's environment):

1. Leadership
2. STEM (Science, Technology, Engineering, and Mathematics) Education
3. Research and Strategic Technology
4. Infrastructure Architecture
5. Digital Architecture
6. Knowledge Management
7. Diplomacy
8. World Currency Gold Standard
9. Electro-Dollar
10. Financial Capital
11. Security
12. Transformative Grand Digital Strategies and Policies

Theodore Roosevelt (Republican president of the United States from 1901 to 1909):

"Get action, do things," was his attitude toward all endeavors, political and otherwise.

Theodore Roosevelt was the youngest person ever to become President of the United States. He was a trailblazer of the progressive movement. Theodore fought for his "Square Deal" national policies, assuring the average equality of citizens, breaking bad trusts, railways, and the purity of food and drugs. He made natural conservation a top priority and established many new national parks, forests, and monuments to preserve the nation's natural resources.

(Modified from Source: Library of Congress Prints and Photographs Division Washington, D.C, under the digital ID ppmsca.35645)

On the foreign policy side, Roosevelt focused on Central America, where he began constructing the Panama Canal. Theodore Roosevelt expanded the US Navy and sent his *Great White Fleet*, a new Naval Force, on a world tour to propel the United States' maritime power. TR's successful efforts to broker the end of the Russo-Japanese War won him the 1906 Nobel Peace Prize.

Franklin D. Roosevelt *(Four-term Democratic President of the United States from 1933 until he died in 1945):*

Even with the Defense Production Act[59], we still have trouble making something as essential but necessary as facemasks in Coronavirus's present age. FDR managed the first year of the nation's supercharged production. The ultra-productive schedule resulted in 45,000 aircraft, 45,000 tanks, 20,000 anti-aircraft guns, and 8 million tons in new ships.

Despite his crippling polio at age 39, he became president at the age of 50. He was our unwavering Commander-in-Chief who steered this country through two large catastrophes (the Great Depression and World War II). FDR served as commander-in-chief longer than any other President. His legacy still shapes our understanding of the role of government and the presidency.

The policies and persona of Franklin D. Roosevelt set the gold standard for the modern presidency. Engendering both respect and contempt, FDR exerted courageous leadership during the most tumultuous period in the nation's history since the Civil War. FDR was elected for a record *four* presidential elections and became a pivotal figure in global events throughout the first half of the 20th century.

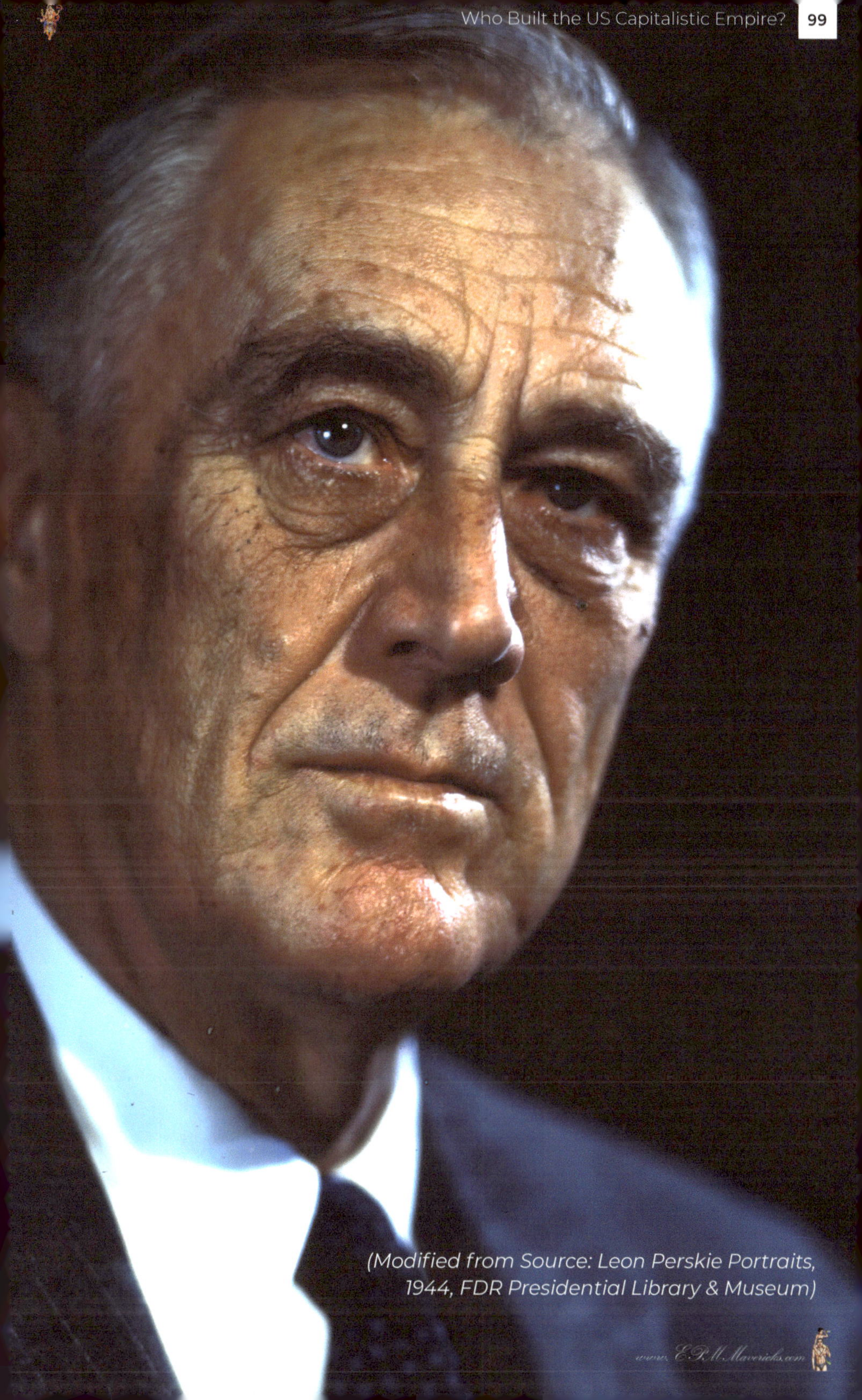

(Modified from Source: Leon Perskie Portraits, 1944, FDR Presidential Library & Museum)

Through the trials of the Great Depression, Roosevelt led the federal government, executing his New Deal domestic program in response to the worst economic crisis in the history of the United States. The governmental "safety net" he created would be his most incredible legacy and a source of ongoing controversy. He is regarded by scholars to be among the nation's greatest presidents after George Washington and Abraham Lincoln.

Eleanor Roosevelt

She was known as the "First Lady of the World." For more than thirty years, Eleanor Roosevelt was America's most powerful woman. Millions adored her, but her FBI file was thicker than a stack of phone books. She fearlessly spoke out for civil rights, and the KKK put a price on her head.

Satirized as an ugly busybody by the media, Eleanor helped Franklin D. Roosevelt rise to power and became his most valuable political asset. She persevered, indifferent to the onslaught of mockery, fighting tirelessly for social justice for all and taking a leading role in the United Nations landmark Declaration of Human Rights.

FDR entered the White House amid the Great Depression, which started in 1929 and lasted approximately a decade. The President and Congress soon implemented a series of recovery initiatives known as the New Deal to combat the economic downturn. Eleanor traveled across the United States as the first lady, acting as her husband's eyes and ears and reporting back to him. President Harry S. Truman later called her the "First Lady of the World" in tribute to her human rights achievements.

"The skillful leader subdues the enemy's troops without any fighting; he captures their cities without laying siege to them; he overthrows their kingdom without lengthy operations in the field."

Sun Tzu's The Art of War (476–221 BC)

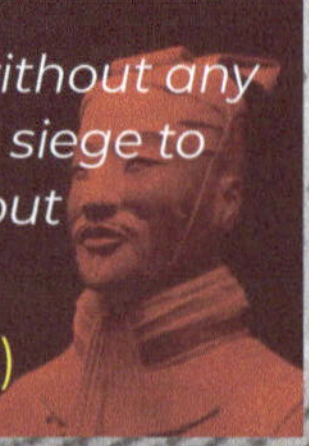

(Modified from Source:
FDR Presidential Library & Museum)

We should revisit our founding capitalistic doctrine from the Roosevelt days:

"At the present moment in world history, nearly every nation must choose between alternative ways of life. The choice is too often not a free one. One way of life is based upon the will of the majority and is distinguished by free institutions, representative government, free elections, guarantees of individual liberty, freedom of speech and religion, and freedom from political oppression. The second way of life is based upon the will of a minority forcibly imposed upon the majority. It relies upon terror and oppression, a controlled press and radio, fixed elections, and the suppression of personal freedoms. I believe that it must be the policy of the United States to support free peoples who are resisting attempted subjugation by armed minorities or by outside pressures.

....

The seeds of totalitarian regimes are nurtured by misery and want. They spread and grow in the evil soil of poverty and strife. They reach their full growth when the hope of a people for a better life has died. We must keep that hope alive. The free peoples of the world look to us for support in maintaining their freedoms. If we falter in our leadership, we may endanger the peace of the world and we shall surely endanger the welfare of our own Nation.”

The Truman Doctrine (1947)

(Image credit: US Army and so PD-USGov-Military-Army)
Yalta summit 1945 with Churchill, Roosevelt, Stalin

A PROPOSAL TO BRING BACK THE HOUSE OF ROOSEVELTS

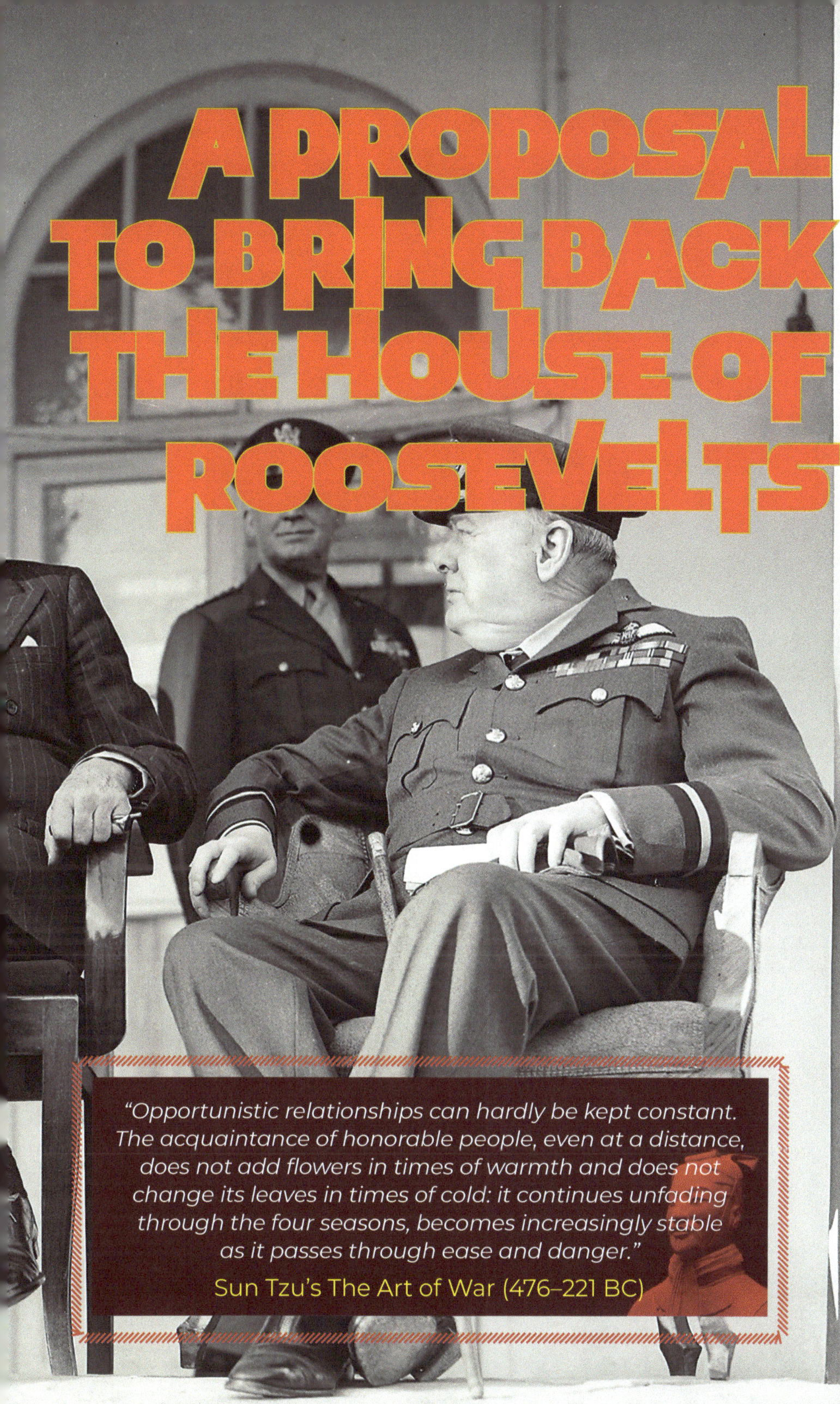

"Opportunistic relationships can hardly be kept constant. The acquaintance of honorable people, even at a distance, does not add flowers in times of warmth and does not change its leaves in times of cold: it continues unfading through the four seasons, becomes increasingly stable as it passes through ease and danger."

Sun Tzu's The Art of War (476–221 BC)

My proposal focuses on strategies we highlighted earlier to revive western enterprises, which are:

1. Leadership
2. Science, Technology, Engineering, and Mathematics (STEM) Education
3. Research and Strategic Technology
4. Infrastructure Architecture
5. Digital Architecture
6. Knowledge Management
7. Diplomacy
8. World Currency Gold Standard
9. Electro-Dollar
10. Financial Capital
11. Security
12. Digital Strategies and Transformative Roadmap

The spider chart below represents a bird's eye view comparison between Roosevelt's capitalist era and today's America, contrasted with the progress the Chinese made. The details will be explained in each section (please let me know your perspectives to consolidate and update these graphs).

With government support, Chinese enterprises effectively colonize the world by financially influencing more than 150 countries with at least $10 trillion worth of debt-trap diplomacy, next-generation Belt & Silk Road, and other high-tech infrastructure projects.

Our current 19th-century capitalistic system is under the leadership of the corrupt PACs and lobbyists in the swamp (Washington DC), Gordon Gekko's Private Equity, and corporate raiders, many of whom are funded by the Chinese. Twitter-driven Wall-Street algorithmic decision-making process is a disgrace. Our enterprise pundits soon become disconnected from the realities of 96% of humanity. They live in an ivory tower and are only concentrating on excessive financial engineering. Hardly any productivity or sales growth has occurred in the past decade. Despite this, the Dow Jones has risen more than 250% in the past ten years, primarily through financial engineering. The get-rich-quick schemes have squandered the significant balance sheet, and now the foundations of capitalism tremble.

★ ★

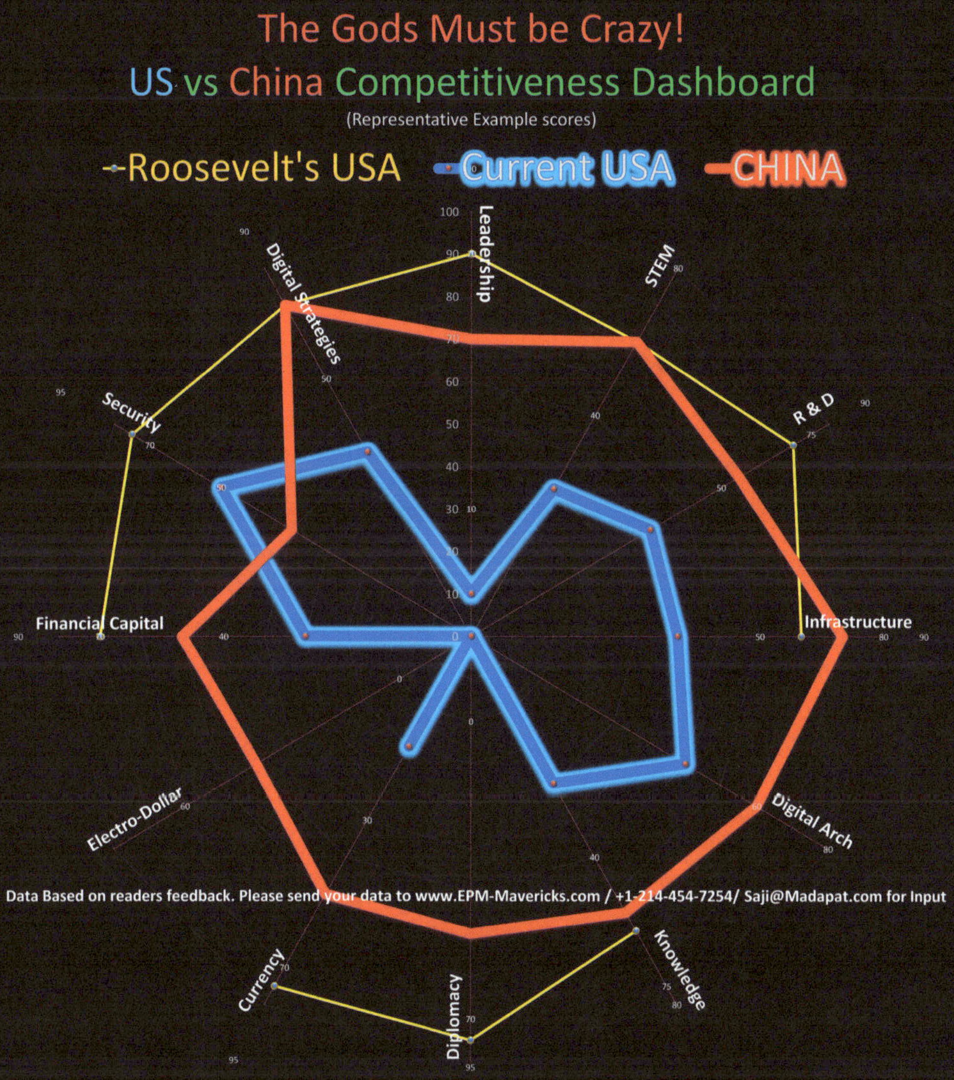

We should reform our enterprises to march into the 22nd century by learning from the best of the Germans and the East (Singapore, China, Japan, South Korea, etc.). Enterprise's survival is intertwined with the rise and fall of its sponsoring godfather empires, as we have witnessed over the past five centuries. Chinese communist party resilience engineers strategically spend trillions of dollars to ruthlessly eliminate many of their western prodigal capitalistic financial engineering masters, especially on 22nd-century generation inventions. Quasi-governmental enterprises have liberated from its legacy western Gordon Gekko license masters and foreign partners for better products and services.

In summary, we need to double down on our enterprise investments in the following areas to liberate ourselves from the new communist authoritarian masters:

Ay Yi Yai Yi! We are in the middle of The New World Order!

1. Leadership

"The skillful leader subdues the enemy's troops without any fighting; he captures their cities without laying siege to them; he overthrows their kingdom without lengthy operations in the field."

Sun Tzu's The Art of War (476–221 BC)

Harvard Kennedy School says, "*As the CCP prepares to celebrate the 100th anniversary of its founding, the Party appears to be as strong as ever. A deeper resilience is founded on popular support for regime policy.*" This research paper on the Chinese Communist Party (CCP) is a series published by the Ash Center for Democratic Governance and Innovation at Harvard University's John F. Kennedy School of Government.

"There is little evidence to support the idea that the CCP is losing legitimacy in the eyes of its people. In fact, our survey shows that, across a wide variety of metrics, by 2016 the Chinese government was more popular than at any point during the previous two decades. On average, Chinese citizens reported that the government's provision of healthcare, welfare, and other essential public services was far better and more equitable than when the survey began in 2003.

****....****

As such, there was no real sign of burgeoning discontent among China's main demographic groups, casting doubt on the idea that the country was facing a crisis of political legitimacy."

Harvard University (July 2020)

Meanwhile, in the US:

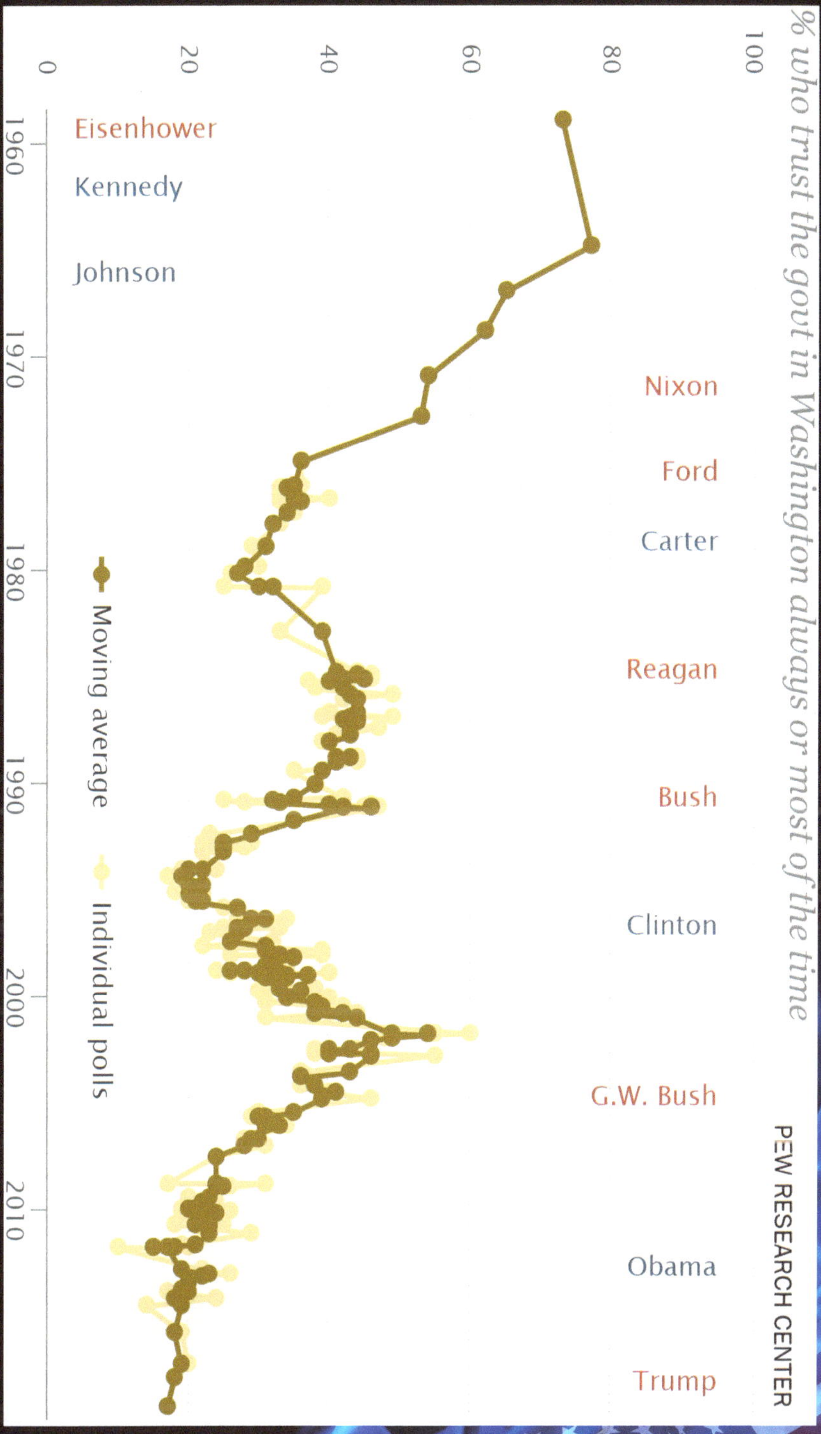
% who trust the govt in Washington always or most of the time
PEW RESEARCH CENTER
100
80
60
40
20
0
1960
1970
1980
1990
2000
2010
Eisenhower
Kennedy
Johnson
Nixon
Ford
Carter
Reagan
Bush
Clinton
G.W. Bush
Obama
Trump
Moving average
Individual polls

> ***"Only 17% of Americans today say they can trust the government in Washington to do what is right "just about always" (3%)"***
>
> — Pew Research Center
>
> (Public Trust in Government: 1958-2019)

As history tends to repeat itself with a vengeance, we must have resilient leadership, such as the Roosevelts, to manage our empire and our enterprise. It is high time for leaders like FDR to emerge. Leaders who can transform the COVID-19 malady into a call for courage, tenacity and hopefulness. FDR was the US's most exceptional leader. He brought us to the forefront of the world-historical stage by building the foundation for capitalism and modern enterprise. We need to pray for visionary leaders, such as the Roosevelts, who will pave the redemption road to the future to lead us back to the shining city upon the hill.

As we go through the existential climate crisis, we need to have prophets such as Theodore Roosevelt (TR), who recognized how important it was to preserve these assets we are so blessed to have. TR created 150 national forests, five national parks, 51 federal bird reserves, four national game preserves, and 18 national monuments on over 230 million acres of public land.

As we muddle through the Black Lives Matter era, let us learn from the "First Lady of the World" (Eleanor Roosevelt), who redefined the nation based on our humanitarian efforts and social justice struggle.

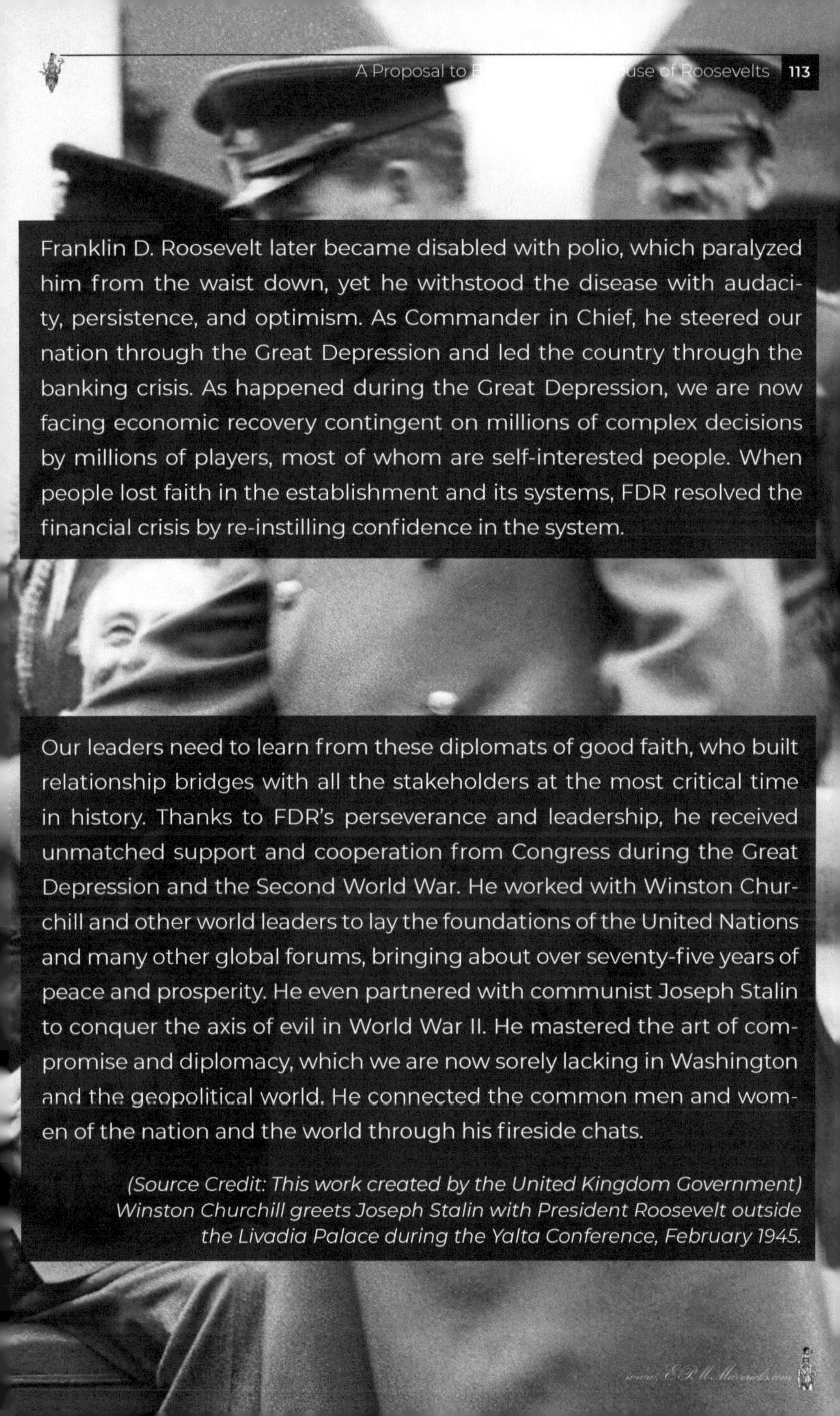

Franklin D. Roosevelt later became disabled with polio, which paralyzed him from the waist down, yet he withstood the disease with audacity, persistence, and optimism. As Commander in Chief, he steered our nation through the Great Depression and led the country through the banking crisis. As happened during the Great Depression, we are now facing economic recovery contingent on millions of complex decisions by millions of players, most of whom are self-interested people. When people lost faith in the establishment and its systems, FDR resolved the financial crisis by re-instilling confidence in the system.

Our leaders need to learn from these diplomats of good faith, who built relationship bridges with all the stakeholders at the most critical time in history. Thanks to FDR's perseverance and leadership, he received unmatched support and cooperation from Congress during the Great Depression and the Second World War. He worked with Winston Churchill and other world leaders to lay the foundations of the United Nations and many other global forums, bringing about over seventy-five years of peace and prosperity. He even partnered with communist Joseph Stalin to conquer the axis of evil in World War II. He mastered the art of compromise and diplomacy, which we are now sorely lacking in Washington and the geopolitical world. He connected the common men and women of the nation and the world through his fireside chats.

(Source Credit: This work created by the United Kingdom Government)
Winston Churchill greets Joseph Stalin with President Roosevelt outside the Livadia Palace during the Yalta Conference, February 1945.

When foundational trials and tribulations threaten our empire and the sandy shores of our enterprise architectures, we need leaders like the Roosevelts, who can rebuild and guide us to the shining city upon the hill by:

1. Inspiring us with a vision, a strategy and a roadmap for our future
2. Leading us with hopefulness and confidence, no matter how uncertain the future is
3. Taking audacious actions with determination and resolve
4. Collaborating with all the stakeholders and even negotiating with our potential enemies to develop a plan for action
5. Executing decisions that benefit the greater good, even if it is not politically correct

It is high time to analyze the Middle Kingdom to assess how well they are playing *their* trump cards. Our time is running out. For our Empire and Enterprise, we need to have noble and intelligent leaders, such as the Roosevelts, who have self-confidence, determination, integrity, and diplomacy, without which we will inevitably falter.

2. STEM Education (Science, Technology, Engineering, and Mathematics)

> *"Deep knowledge is to be aware of disturbance before disturbance, to be aware of danger before danger, to be aware of destruction before destruction, to be aware of calamity before calamity. Strong action is training the body without being burdened by the body, exercising the mind without being used by the mind, working in the world without being affected by the world, carrying out tasks without being obstructed by tasks."*
>
> Sun Tzu's The Art of War (476–221 BC)

The quality of education has formed the backbone of empires throughout history. A strong education is the backbone of growth. Based on the 2015 PISA test scores, the United States already ranks in the 15th lowest percentile of the developed world.

Unfortunately, public education and school funding are the lowest-hanging fruits for budget cuts, especially in the post-COVID era. STEM education is the most expensive of all and the most natural prey for budget slashing. On top of that, the current economic situation has led to high unemployment rates, which leads to instability in the home, ultimately resulting in poor academic results, a lack of opportunities, and a depressed income. These factors develop a vicious cycle that leads to socio-economic and geopolitical instabilities around the world.

In the current political environment, education has become the last priority. In addition to policy changes, we must investigate creative solutions, such as partnerships between philanthropy, government, and business, to address these kinds of challenges. We must establish public-private partnerships similar to the German technical and vocational education and training (TVET).

Like in Singapore, Germany, China, Japan, South Korea, and India, the government must take an active leadership role in public education. The government should reward and recognize teachers based on their performance. As it stands, the United States certifies significantly fewer undergraduate engineers annually than China or even India.

According to the OECD (Organization for Economic Cooperation and Development) 2018 report, the US spends more on college than almost any other country. "The expenses per student is exorbitant, and it has virtually no relationship to the value that students could get in exchange."[60]

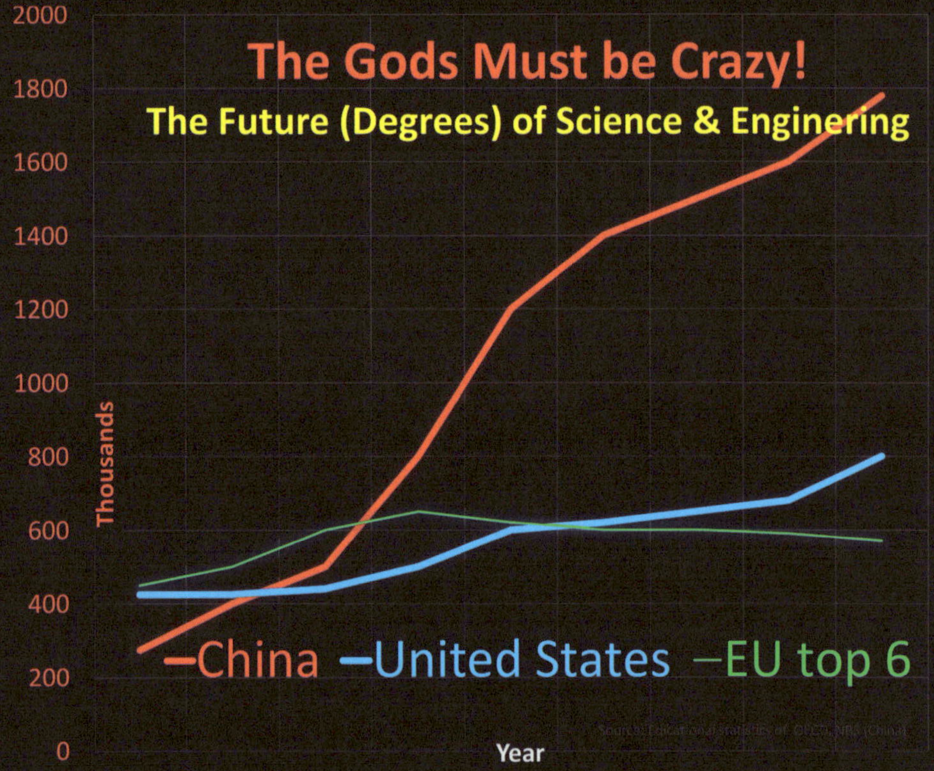

★ ★

Decadence is to blame - fancy student apartments, expensive meals, and "the mania for athletic sports." We need to transform the education system and begin partnerships with philanthropists such as Bill Gates and Bloomberg to train and prepare the workforce for the 22nd century. As an example, in IT:

- ★ IT/Business systems must evolve from Transactional–>Operational–>Predictive Analytics AI BOTs (Robotic Automation in Cloud)
- ★ In addition to IT, traditional Accounting and most business functions (especially repetitive ones) are on the verge of automation by AI BOTs in the cloud

Our workforce must be AI-ready, as Robotics Automation and AI will be necessary evils for productivity and economic growth. Millions of people worldwide will need to switch occupations or upgrade skills. Mckinsey estimates that *between 400 million and 800 million individuals could be under displacement by automation and need to find new jobs by 2030. Of the total displaced, 75 million to 375 million may need to switch occupational categories and learn new skills.*

3. Research and Strategic Technology

> *"If you know the enemy and know yourself, you need not fear the result of a hundred battles. If you know yourself but not the enemy, for every victory gained you will also suffer a defeat. If you know neither the enemy nor yourself, you will succumb in every battle."*
>
> Sun Tzu's The Art of War (476–221 BC)

Has America's most valuable company lost its mojo? Besides the stock buybacks and milking the ancient iPhones, technologically generations behind the competitors from the east, what innovations has Apple brought in the past decade? Apple appears to have died with Steve Jobs.

Our unicorns in Silicon Valley are venturing out, especially to the east. It appears Silicon Valley has lost its way, too.

"Venture capital and tech start-up economy are creating a dangerous, "high stakes Ponzi scheme" and a "bizarre Ponzi balloon."

Chamath Palihapitiya

(Billionaire investor and former Facebook Vice President of User Growth)

The Chinese are at the forefront of the technological frontier in common areas such as electronics, machinery, automobiles, high-speed railways, and aviation. Rather, they are also driving technological innovations in emerging areas such as 5G, renewable energy, advanced nuclear energy, next-generation telecommunication technologies, big data and super-computers, AI, robotics, space technology, and electronic commerce.

In 2018, the Chinese filed almost 50% of the patent applications worldwide, with a record of 1.54 million in high technology. Compare that with the United States, which filed less than 600,000. China's Artificial Intelligence patent filing levels overtook the US in 2014, and China has since maintained a high growth rate.

Most Chinese leaders are engineers thinking from a strategic long-term resilience and value perspective, rather than extremely short-term financial engineering shortcuts. They prioritize and focus on long-term 22nd-century technologies, including artificial intelligence, cloud computing, big data analytics, blockchain, and information communications technology (ICT).

As the Chinese Digital Silk Road expands, its pseudo-enterprises will have priceless insights into the data globally. Much like how FAANGs (Facebook, Apple, Amazon, Netflix, and Google) use real-time data ag-

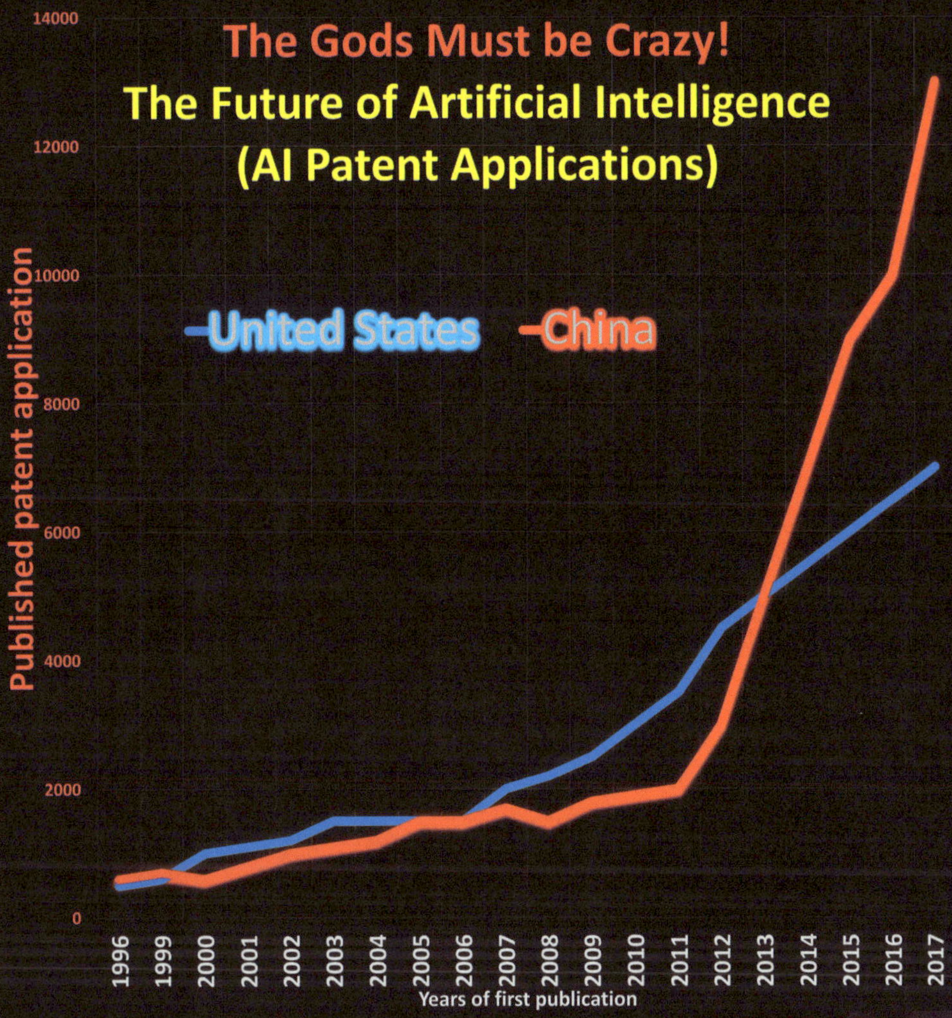

★ ★

gregation to analyze the West's customer behavior. Being associated with the Chinese government, they will have privileged access to all the Middle Kingdom subjects, unlike their western competitors. These Chinese quasi-enterprises will have extraordinary privileges in the next frontier technologies like IoT (Internet of Things), AI (artificial intelligence), and autonomous vehicles to at least two-thirds of the world through the DSR platform.

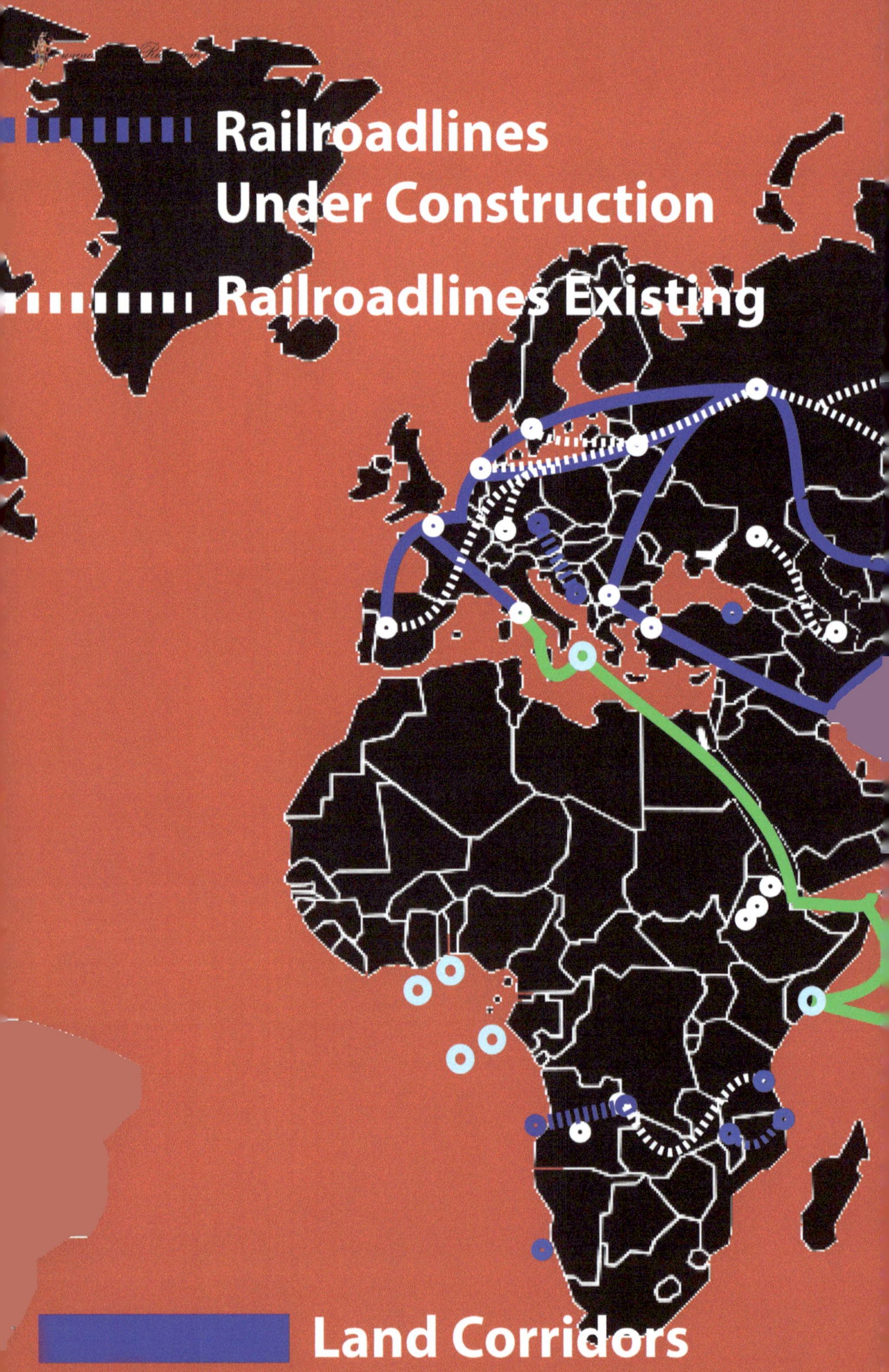
Railroadlines
Under Construction
Railroadlines Existing
Land Corridors

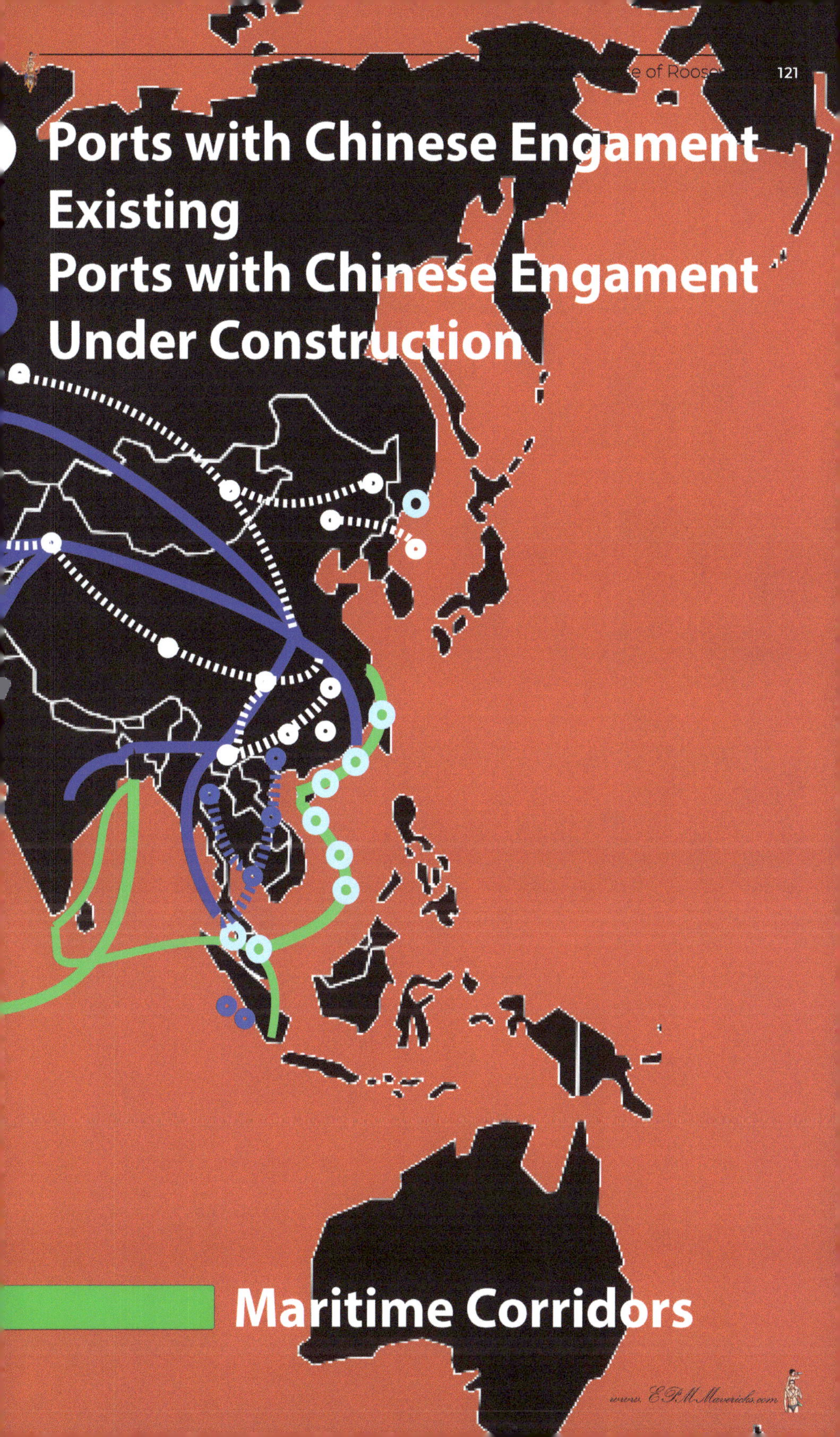
Ports with Chinese Engament
Existing
Ports with Chinese Engament
Under Construction
Maritime Corridors

Unfortunately, in the west, today's enterprise architectures and technologies that predate the WWW (World Wide Web) are run by "lipstick on a pig" specialist financial engineers. Their designs have no relation to the digital age. As happened with the Roosevelts, through public-private partnerships, universities should invest and nurture the core industries, similar to what we see happening in China, Japan, South Korea, and Germany.

4. Infrastructure Architecture

> *"The general who wins a battle makes many calculations in his temple before the battle is fought. The general who loses a battle makes but few calculations.*
>
> Sun Tzu's The Art of War (476–221 BC)

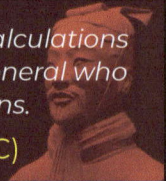

To survive, we need to draft a modern version of the 'New Deal' that Franklin D. Roosevelt executed a century ago under similar circumstances. Just as he did, we must apply significant investments to our dilapidated infrastructure.

As China seeks to colonize economically, we must examine our progressive version of the Global Marshall Plan to counter China's Belt & Road and technological infrastructure.

- ★ We need to reinvigorate entrepreneurship through public-private partnerships and universities.
- ★ The government should take equity ownership in strategic enterprises, helping them to recover.

- ★ The government should monitor private equity firms and venture capitalists in critical industries, especially in Silicon Valley. Considerable predatory funding is coming from China intent on stealing our IP, which is a potential threat to our national security interest.
- ★ We must scrap the obsolete immigration system and focus on merit. Many of our innovative high-tech leaders are the result of high-end immigration.
- ★ As Roosevelt did, we must break up the monopolies and too-big-to-fail corporations that create barriers to innovation.

"Small and medium-sized enterprises (SMEs) make up over 99% of the total number of businesses across the countries where we work. They are responsible for large contributions to value added and employment."

——— The European Bank for Reconstruction and Development (EBRD) ———

5. Digital Architecture

"First lay plans which will ensure victory, and then lead your army to battle; if you will not begin with stratagem but rely on brute strength alone, victory will no longer be assured"

"Let your plans be dark and impenetrable as night, and when you move, fall like a thunderbolt."

Sun Tzu's The Art of War (476–221 BC)

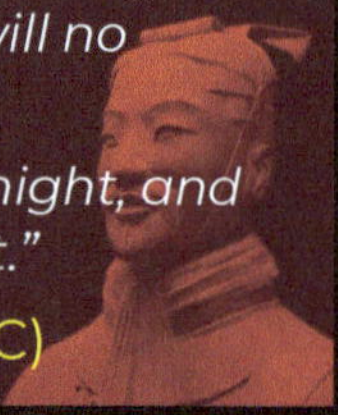

"We must seize the opportunities afforded by industrial digitalization and digital industrialization, accelerate the construction of new infrastructures such as 5G networks and data centers, and step up the layout of strategic emerging industries and future industries such as the digital economy, life and health, and new materials."

— Xi Jinping, General Secretary of the Communist Party of China —

China has already signed Digital Silk Road specific agreements with many of its existing Belt and Road Initiative (BRI) partner countries. DSR is a Trojan Horse for Beijing to enhance its influence around the world without competition. It is a digital backdoor for Chinese technology companies such as Huawei, Tencent, and Alibaba to expand their global business footprints and torpedo their western competitors.

China's Global Infrastructure Footprint

While we are stuck in 2G/3G/4G wars, China leaps its 5G expansion mode and is now looking at 6G. Over a year ago, China granted operating licenses to China Mobile, China Unicom, and China Telecom. In 2019, these state-owned telecom enterprises began rolling out 5G networks in cities across the country. Starting from 50K base stations in 2019, China has already crossed half a billion 5G subscriptions. It added at least 190k new 5G base stations in the first half of 2021 alone[61]

Carrier	5G subs total (millions)	New 5G subs in 2021 (millions)	5G base stations	New 5G base stations 2021	Total subscribers (millions)
China Mobile	251	86	501,000	111,000	946
China Unicom	121	42.2	460,000	80,000	310
China Telecom	131	44.5	460,000	80,000	362
Totals	503	172.7	1,421,000*	271,000	1,618

Source: https://www.theregister.com/2021/08/20/china_5g_progress/

China owns or assists in the construction of ~30% of current cables in Asia and is targeting more than 50% of the shares shortly. Huawei 5G is more cutting-edge than western competitor networks and is marketing it cheaply to the rest of the world. The Chinese satellite navigation system has more satellites than the USA aligned GPS navigation system. At least thirty Belt and Road Initiative (BRI) countries already signed for the BeiDou navigation network.

Beyond economic colonization, as China seeks to colonize digitally, we must examine our progressive version of the Global *digital* Marshall Plan to counter China's Belt & Road and technological infrastructure.

It will be a Herculean task for western enterprises to catch up with state-funded monolithic Chinese quasi-enterprises such as Alibaba, Huawei, Tencent, and ZTE, which deliver state-of-the-art products at a throw-away price, thanks to subsidies.

5. Knowledge Management

> *"Regard your soldiers as your children, and they will follow you into the deepest valleys; look upon them as your own beloved sons, and they will stand by you even unto death. If, however, you are indulgent, but unable to make your authority felt; kind-hearted, but unable to enforce your commands; and incapable, moreover, of quelling disorder: then your soldiers must be likened to spoilt children; they are useless for any practical purpose."*
>
> Sun Tzu's The Art of War (476–221 BC)

Vhat we need today is high-tech and resilient engineering – not finan-ial engineering that serves only to squander what we already have. The productivity of an enterprise's knowledge resources, their employees, is he key to its success. Knowledge management is under the control of a ulture of teamwork, learning, and inventiveness. Team empowerment eads to knowledge enterprise, which is the foundation for the future f the organization. Sadly, in today's environment, knowledge resourc-s are the primary casualty. They receive the same treatment as liability ost centers, which has resulted in the current unemployment figure of round forty million.

Knowledge resources are the backbone of enterprises – not liabilities.

> *"The skillful employer of men will employ the wise man, the brave man, the covetous man, and the stupid man. For the wise man delights in establishing his merit, the brave man likes to show his courage in action, the covetous man is quick at seizing advantages, and the stupid man has no fear of death."*
>
> Sun Tzu's The Art of War (476–221 BC)

Evolution of Knowledge Enterprise

"90% of the knowledge in the organization is in the heads of the people. Management spends75 % of their time on the knowledge that is written down."
- Bob Buckman

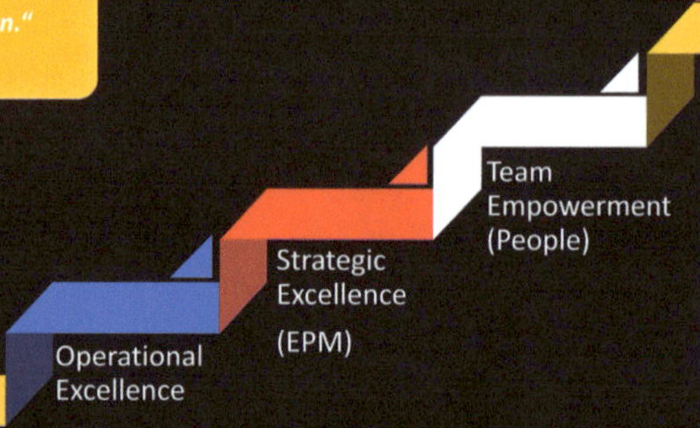

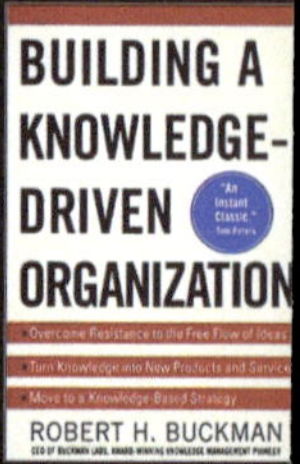

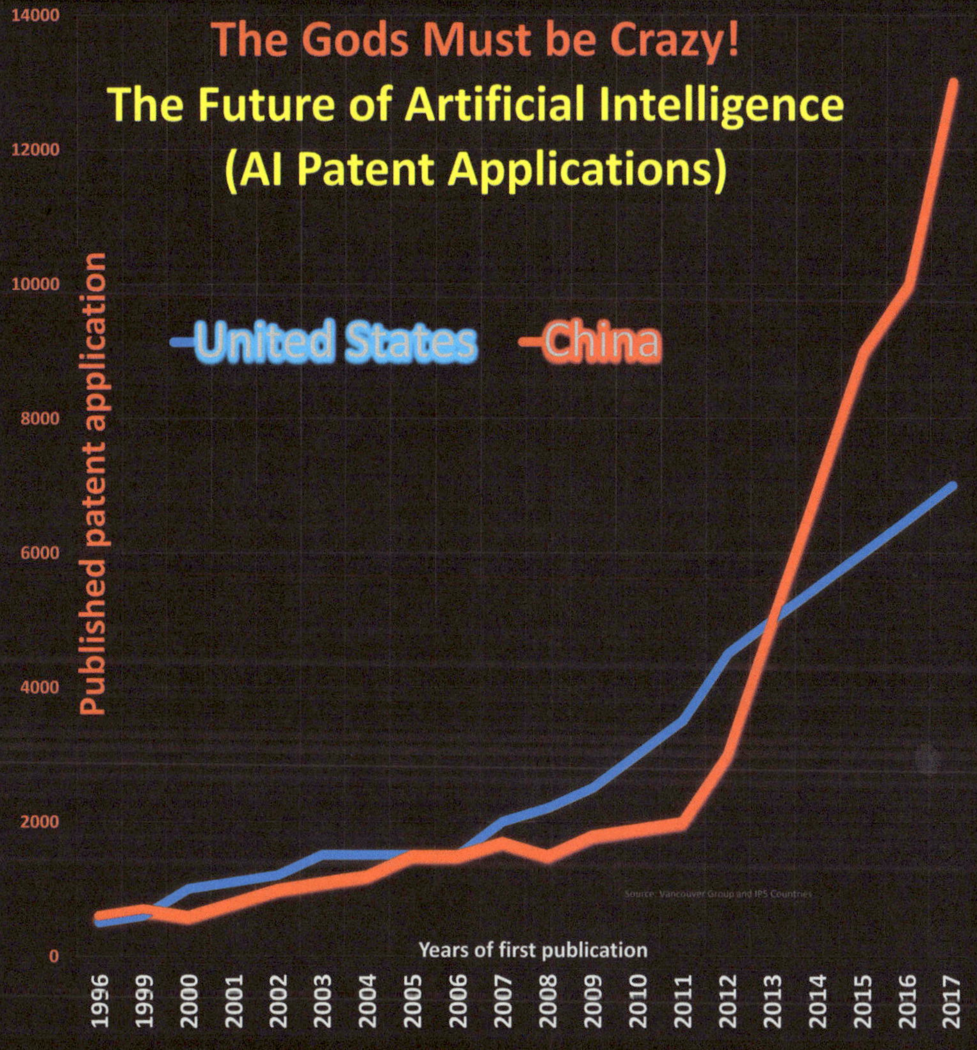
The Gods Must be Crazy!
The Future of Artificial Intelligence
(AI Patent Applications)
United States
China
Published patent application
14000
12000
10000
8000
6000
4000
2000
0
Source: Vancouver Group and IPS Countries
Years of first publication
1996
1999
2000
2001
2002
2003
2004
2005
2006
2007
2008
2009
2010
2011
2012
2013
2014
2015
2016
2017

7. Diplomacy

"Keep your friends close and your enemies closer."
Sun Tzu's The Art of War (476–221 BC)

Today, we need to build diplomatic bridges and tear down the walls, not build them. Instead of withdrawing and letting China take the lead, we should surge forward to retake the lead by completely revamping our trade alliances such as WTO, World Bank, IMF, UN, and WHO, which Roosevelt established immediately after World War II. We need to secure the Trans-Pacific Partnership (TPP) leadership and prepare it to take steps to counter China. The Trans-Pacific Partnership Agreement was a proposed trade agreement between Australia, Brunei, Canada, Chile, Japan, Malaysia, Mexico, New Zealand, Peru, Singapore, Vietnam, and the United States, signed into effect in 2016. Unfortunately, the previous administration under President Trump withdrew from the partnership in 2017, and China took advantage of the US withdrawal.

During the Roosevelt years, the US was the most respected country globally, with the most net international investment positions (in terms of GDP percent). The United States owned more foreign assets than foreigners held of its own, until around the 1980s. Since the 1990s, thanks to its decadent and expensive lifestyle, the US has been selling its prized assets to foreigners.

As of 2016, China (124) is a top trading partner of most countries. That number is more than twice that of the US (56). Concerningly, American ambassadorships are on sale to wealthy donors. Typical presidential campaigns cost billions of dollars, and everything is on sale for the rich and powerful. We spend around 5,000% more on the defense budget than on the State Department. Quoting Robert Gates (former defense secretary), "*there are more military marching bands than the makeup of the entire US foreign service.*"

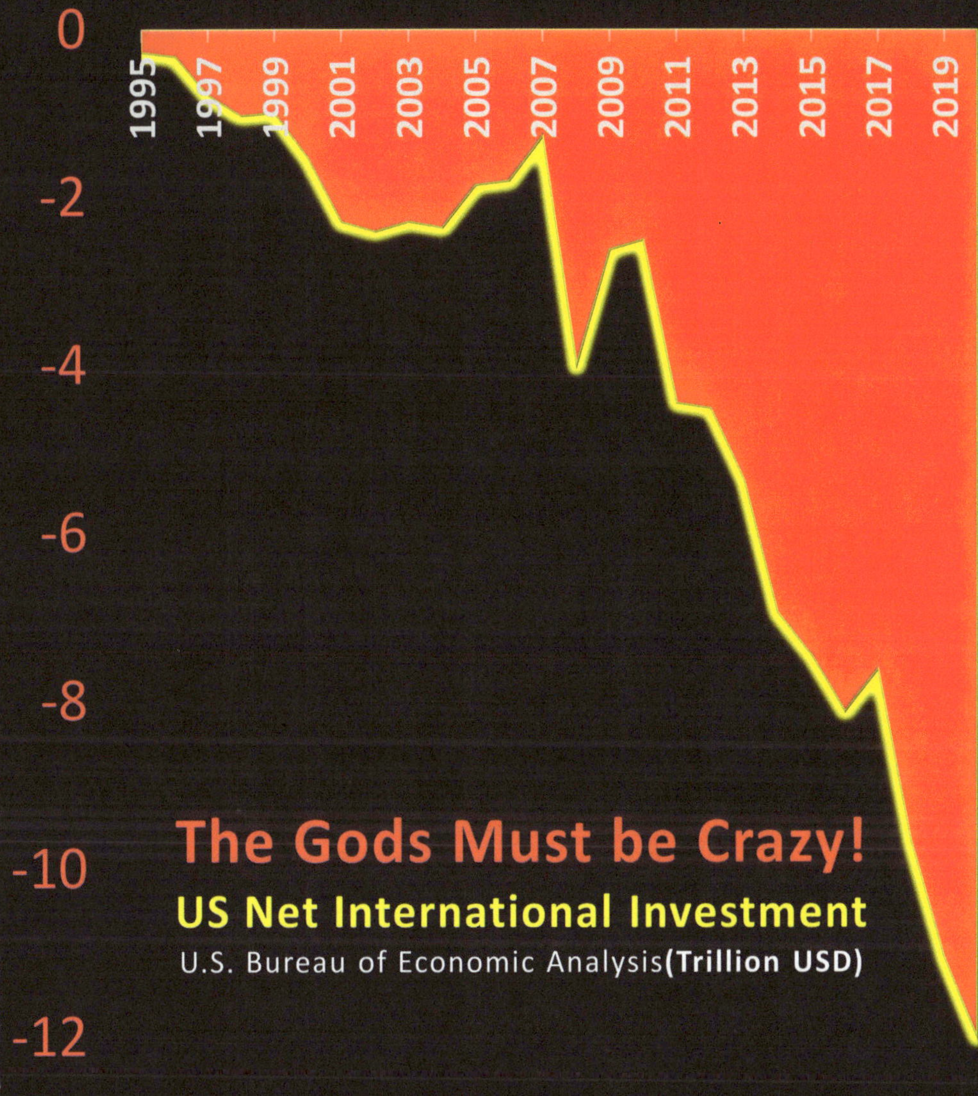
0
-2
-4
-6
-8
-10
-12
1995
1997
1999
2001
2003
2005
2007
2009
2011
2013
2015
2017
2019
The Gods Must be Crazy!
US Net International Investment
U.S. Bureau of Economic Analysis(Trillion USD)

"Opportunistic relationships can hardly be kept constant. The acquaintance of honorable people, even at a distance, does not add flowers in times of warmth and does not change its leaves in times of cold: it continues unfading through the four seasons, becomes increasingly stable as it passes through ease and danger."

Sun Tzu's The Art of War (476–221 BC)

The US used to be very powerful because the rest of the world trusted us as the custodian of trade relationships. Thus, they gave us the privileged reserve currency printing press. If we squander those trade relationships, the Middle Kingdom will soon seize that privilege for their own.

The US had better relations and exported more products and services than it imported until around the 1970s. Regrettably, we lost our trade diplomacy mojo over the past two decades, becoming an isolated dumping ground, especially for China, as depicted in the graph below.

8. World Currency Gold Standard

"Creating a winning war is like balancing a coin of gold against a coin of silver. Creating a losing war is like balancing a coin of silver against a coin of gold."

Sun Tzu's The Art of War (476–221 BC)

Reserve currencies give our enterprise the "godly privilege" of borrowing more money at a lower cost. It also allows us to exert enormous power over all USD financial activities taking place globally, such as controlling the regimes in Iran, Venezuela, and North Korea. Thanks to Roosevelt, the US dollar became the world's reserve currency in 1944. At the time, the US was the most influential country economically, financially, and militarily. However, the high power of reserve currency comes with even greater responsibilities.

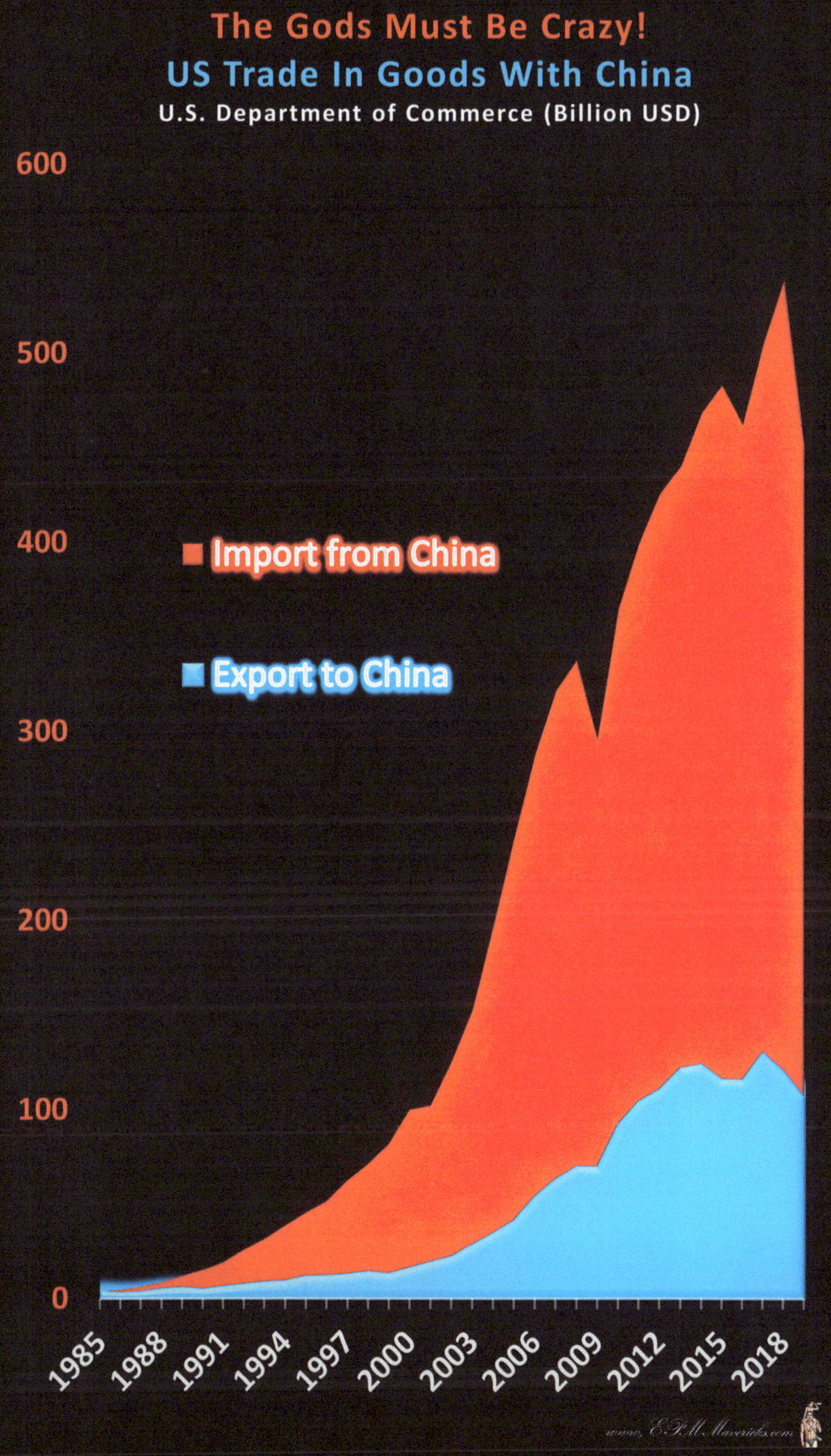
The Gods Must Be Crazy!
US Trade In Goods With China
U.S. Department of Commerce (Billion USD)
600
500
400
300
200
100
0
Import from China
Export to China
1985
1988
1991
1994
1997
2000
2003
2006
2009
2012
2015
2018
www.EPM.Mavericks.com

Seventy-five years ago, the US Economy was around 40% of the World's GDP. Alas, today it is less than 15% in PPP. Meanwhile, China is roaring forward to over 20%. Our abuse of reserve currency custodian privilege has squandered our goodwill. We must reevaluate current methods, or else our empire's days are numbered.

Luckily, 79.5% of all world trade is still conducted in US dollars, thanks to its reserve status[63]. Instead of abusing reserve currency as a political tool and printing it without limits, we should regain trust in the US dollar as reserve currency before it loses its status to Renminbi and its crypto-currency. We need to modernize the IMF, World Bank, and our banking system in line with the emergence of Chinese Financial centers and their cryptocurrencies. Much like the world's universal language remains English, reserve currencies tend to have more staying power because the habit of usage lasts a little longer. Nevertheless, sooner or later, once the rest of the world is susceptible to trade in the Chinese Yuan, its glitter will fade. Facebook, also drooling to digitally colonize its addicts with its Electro-Dollar (Libra cryptocurrency).

9. Electro-Dollar

"In the midst of chaos, there is also opportunity."

Sun Tzu's The Art of War (476–221 BC)

For over 75 years, both directly and indirectly, the United States has controlled most of the world's finances. We have this influence because of our reserve status and our control over institutions like the Society for Worldwide Interbank Financial Telecommunication (SWIFT).

In 2019, the European special-purpose vehicle (SPV) set up trade Exchanges (INSTEX) to facilitate non-USD and non-SWIFT transactions with Iran to avoid breaking US sanctions. INSTEX is a form of a barter

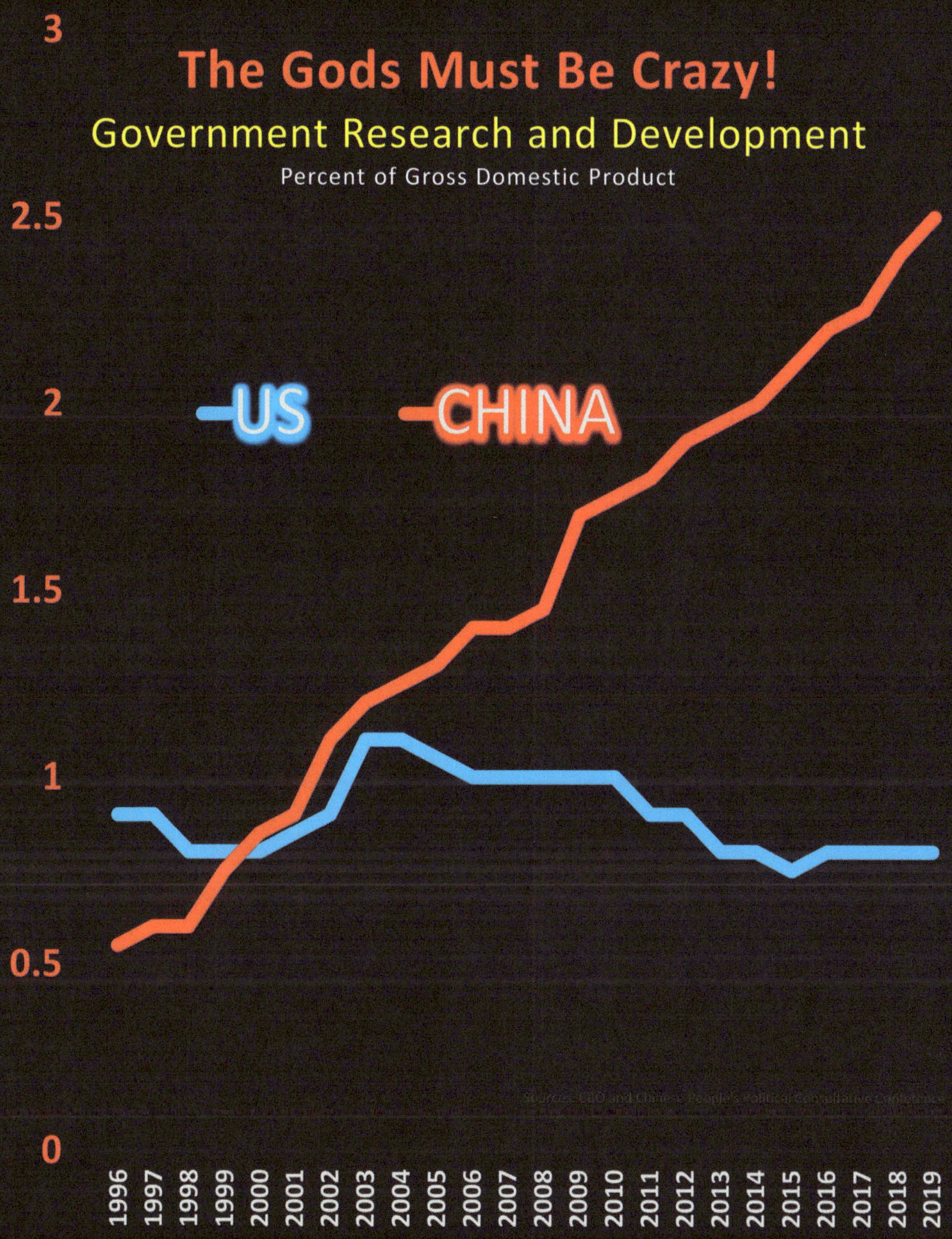
The Gods Must Be Crazy!
Government Research and Development
Percent of Gross Domestic Product
3
2.5
2
1.5
1
0.5
0
US
CHINA
Sources: CBO and Chinese People's Political Consultative Conference
1996
1997
1998
1999
2000
2001
2002
2003
2004
2005
2006
2007
2008
2009
2010
2011
2012
2013
2014
2015
2016
2017
2018
2019

system that allows companies in the European Union, and potentially the rest of the world, to bypass the US financial system by eliminating SWIFT based cross-border payments in USD. When three significant long-term allies of the US (Germany, France, and the UK) are doing this currently to trade with Iran, it is a dangerous warning shot. We should recognize it as a threat not just against the US policies, but as a harbinger of the end to our reserve status. The trade deal between China and Iran can also be settled in the Renminbi, and many other countries, like India will also follow this lead soon. Although China is a closed society, it has an open business attitude, and it studies the US system extensively before making its strategic moves. It seems our open capitalistic society is moving towards extreme closed-mindedness. We are irresponsible with our exceptionalism and lack of long-term strategic thinking entirely. It is high time for us to acknowledge our strategic partners who helped us become a superpower.

Since the 2008 economic tsunami, China has lost faith in western institutions and has begun looking at alternative solutions. They created the Cross-Border Interbank Payment System (CIPS). China established alternative China-based mega financial institutions such as the Asia Infrastructure Investment Bank (AIIB) and the New Development Bank (NDB, previously known as BRICS Bank) as an alternative to the IMF and World Bank founded by the US. The Chinese have also developed more advanced digital payment systems such as WeChat and Alipay, which boast about two billion active users and will exponentially grow once they roll out through the Digital Silk Road (DSR) platform.

While we were battling COVID-19 and civil unrest, the Chinese launched the Blockchain Service Network (BSN). This "digital yuan" is the world's largest blockchain ecosystem, making China the first major economy to issue a national Electro-Yuan (digital currency). The Blockchain Service Network (BSN) is known as the *infrastructure of infrastructures*. This permissionless distributed blockchain ecosystem enables the vertical integration of big data, 5G communications, industrial IoT, cloud comput-

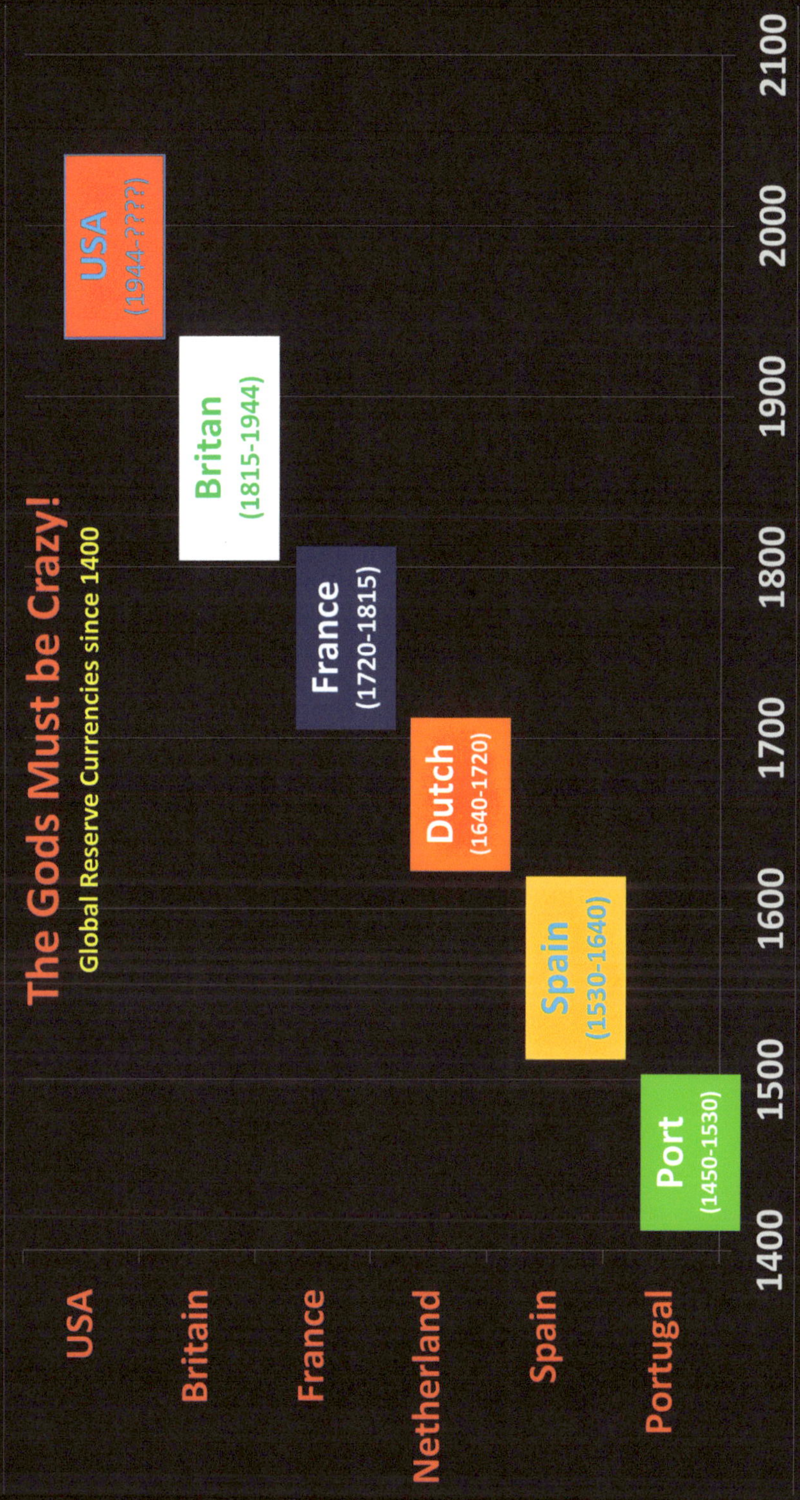
The Gods Must be Crazy!
Global Reserve Currencies since 1400
USA
Britain
France
Netherland
Spain
Portugal
Port (1450-1530)
Spain (1530-1640)
Dutch (1640-1720)
France (1720-1815)
Britan (1815-1944)
USA (1944-????)
1400
1500
1600
1700
1800
1900
2000
2100

ing, and Artificial Intelligence. This financial technology will also provide various other application lever services. The Blockchain Service Network (BSN) has been the main target as the economic nerve of the Digital Silk Road (DSR) by establishing the platform for interconnectivity with all of China's Belt and Road Initiative partners.

Based on a report from JPMorgan, *"There is no country with more to lose from the disruptive potential of digital currency than the United States."* Unfortunately, our outdated financial platform run by Wall Street is ripe for digital disruption. If we do not take immediate action, the Chinese will mercilessly conquer the outdated system built over 75 years ago.

10. Financial Capital

> *"He who wishes to fight must first count the cost."*
> Sun Tzu's The Art of War (476–221 BC)

New York was once the financial nerve center of the world, serving as the free world's responsible engineers. Unfortunately, due to extreme financial engineering, New York is becoming the catacomb of capitalism.

On the other hand, China is rapidly developing its financial center out of Shanghai, which is steadily toppling the influence of the US. The number of public companies in the US has steadily been declining since peaking in the late 90s. This number has shrunk from over 7,000 to less than 3,000 today[64]. Again, the number results from our financial engineering through private equity, mergers and acquisitions, and capital outflows.

Meanwhile, during the same period, the Chinese stock market grew from ZERO to close to 5,000 companies. In the US, this figure dropped by more than 50%. Meanwhile, China has seen a 1000% growth rate in the past 25 years.

The Gods Must be Crazy!
Catacomb of Capitalism?
US Enterprises Black Hole?

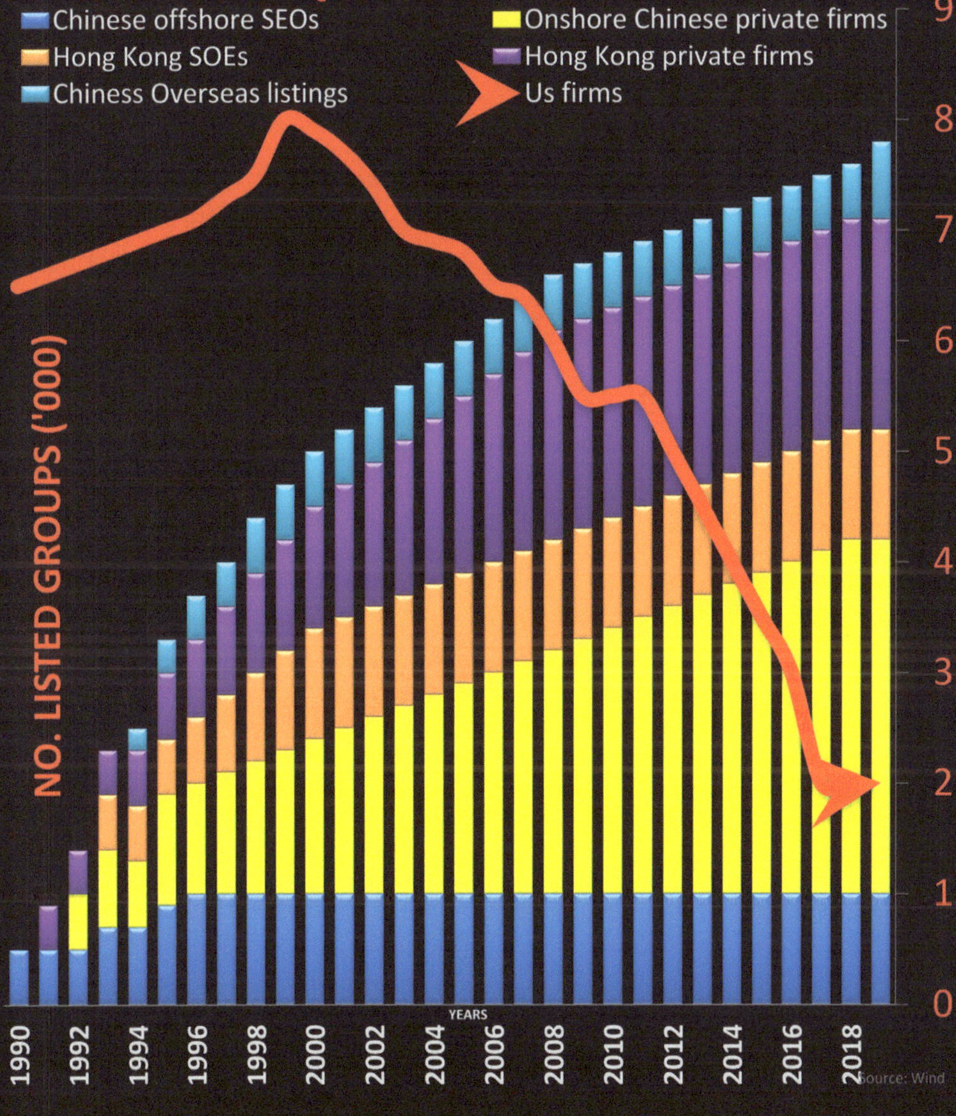

"I have three treasures that I keep and prize: one is kindness, second is frugality, and third is not presuming to take precedence over others. By kindness one can be brave, by frugality one can reach out, and by not presuming to take precedence one can survive effectively. If one gives up kindness and courage, gives up frugality and breadth, and gives up humility for aggressiveness, one will die. The exercise of kindness in battle leads to victory, the exercise of kindness in defense leads to security."

Sun Tzu's The Art of War (476–221 BC)

The mess of our current dog-eat-dog capitalist system lies at the feet of Political Action Committees and lobbyists out of Washington DC. Many private equity firms and other investment vehicles are funded by China and other sovereign wealth funds from foreign countries, which may not have our best interests in mind. Corporate raiders and Gordon Gekko type vultures are looking for quick money. The vast majority of these trades are done between computers and based on algorithms without any fundamentals. They are a disgrace. To retain and sustain, firstly, we should ban the PACs (Political Action Committees). The revolving door between politicians and lobbyists in the swamp (Washington DC) who corrupt and abuse the system should be under investigation.

- ★ We should take the lead in building multi-lateral financial institutions similar to the Asian Infrastructure Investment Bank (AIIB) to counter China's $10 trillion worth of debt-trap diplomacy, next-generation Belt & Silk Road, and other high-tech infrastructure projects. Instead of focusing internally, as Chinese companies do, we need to venture out of our respective ivory towers' comfort zones and expand into new frontiers, especially in emerging countries, for our very survival.

- We should study the impact of Wall Street Quarterly results, share buybacks, and Gordon Gekko investment banking and private equity deals. The government should closely monitor such cancerous activities.
- We should also introduce long-term, performance-based bonuses for executives – not based on short-term share price, which squanders the foundations of an excellent balance sheet.
- Moreover, we should ban the vulture private equity, and sovereign wealth funds. They tend to sacrifice their prey's great balance sheets for their short-term greed.

11. Security

"There are five essentials for victory:
1. He will win who knows when to fight and when not to fight.
2. He will win who knows how to handle both superior and inferior forces.
3. He will win whose army is animated by the same spirit throughout all its ranks.
4. He will win who, prepared himself, waits to take the enemy unprepared.
5. He will win who has military capacity and is not interfered with by the sovereign."

Sun Tzu's The Art of War (476–221 BC)

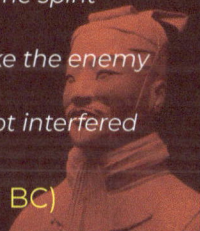

We are still a bunch of warring tribal Bushmen who happen to wear fancy suits and shiny shoes. Governance between 195 countries is challenging, and organizations like the UN, WTO, and more are primarily figureheads. The raw power and might of the gun matter the most. Our superpower status and our military-industrial complexes are critical to protecting our trade routes and enterprises from foreign influence worldwide and even in space. The US military has bases in 70 countries, which is essential to safeguarding our enterprise interests as well.

For four centuries, the Dutch and British East India companies ruled the world from two tiny nations by the might of the gun.

> ***"The West won the world not by the superiority of its ideas or values or religion ... But rather by its superiority in applying organized violence. Westerners often forget this fact; non-Westerners never do."***
>
> — Samuel P. Huntington, The Clash of Civilizations and the Remaking of World Order

While I am no military expert, I have been a consultant in the Aerospace Defense sector for the past several years. Based on the Brown University study (PROFITS OF WAR: CORPORATE BENEFICIARIES OF THE POST-9/11 PENTAGON SPENDING SURGE)[65], nearly half the $14 trillion spent by the Pentagon since 9/11 went to Military Industry complex for-profit defense contractors. These contractors dedicated over one for every member of Congress (about 700 lobbyists) and spent $2.5 billion. This trend originated with then-Vice President Dick Cheney, the former CEO of Halliburton. Halliburton received billions to help set up and run bases, feed troops, and carry out other work in Iraq and Afghanistan by 2008. About one-third of this Pentagon contract was tendered to just five major corporations (Lockheed Martin, Boeing, General Dynamics, Raytheon, and Northrop Grumman). Some of these corporations are owned by sovereign wealth funds, including Saudi Arabia[66], potentially involved in the 911 attacks[67]. The Commission on Wartime Contracting in Iraq and Afghanistan estimated $30B to 60B dollars of waste, fraud, and abuse in 2011 alone. As the US military is withdrawing from Iraq and Afghanistan, now China is their target to justify nearly a trillion-dollar US Defense spending every year. According to the report, "Any member of Congress who doesn't vote for the funds we need to defend this country will be looking for a new job after next November."

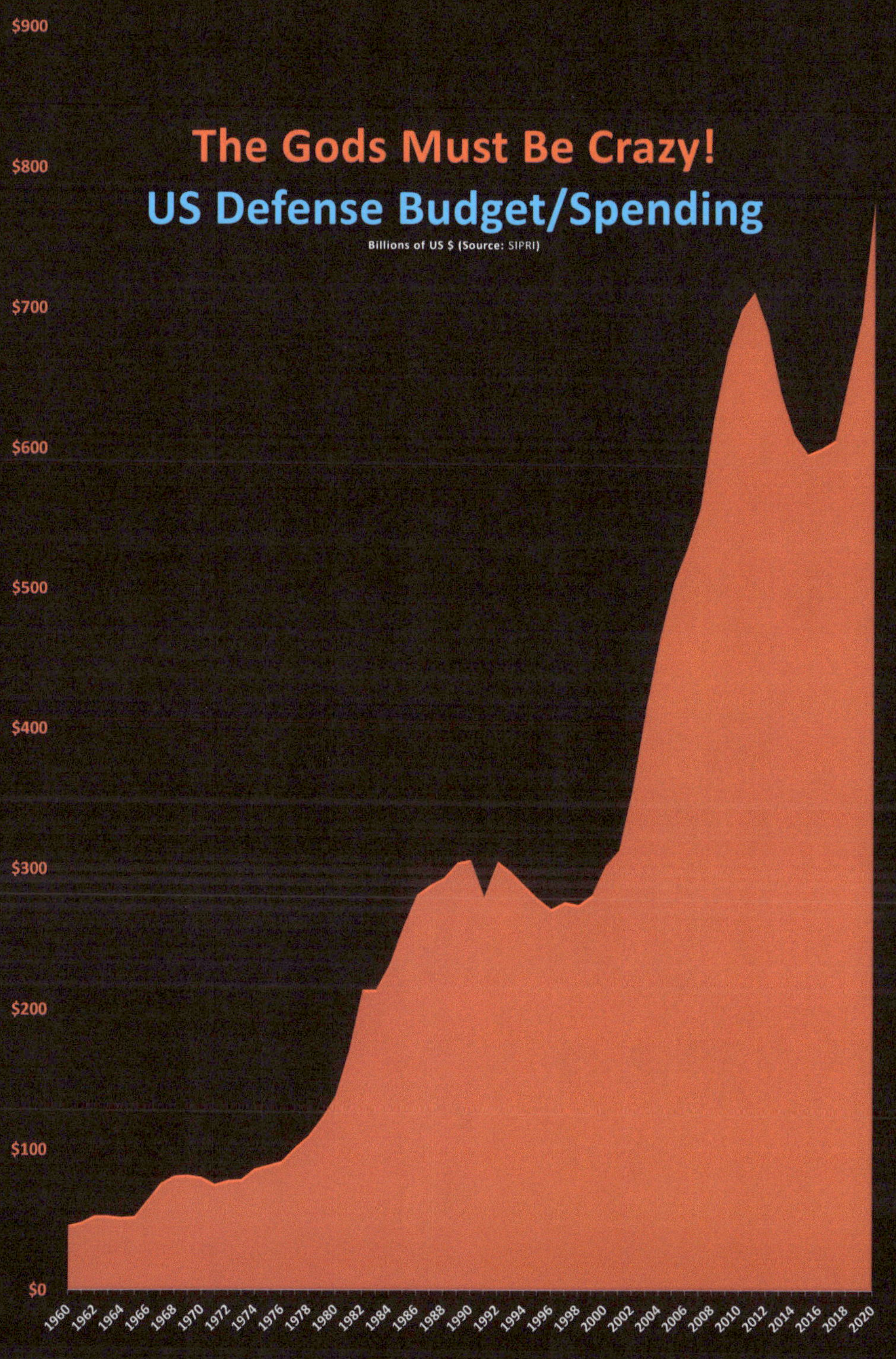
The Gods Must Be Crazy!
US Defense Budget/Spending
Billions of US $ (Source: SIPRI)
$900
$800
$700
$600
$500
$400
$300
$200
$100
$0
1960
1962
1964
1966
1968
1970
1972
1974
1976
1978
1980
1982
1984
1986
1988
1990
1992
1994
1996
1998
2000
2002
2004
2006
2008
2010
2012
2014
2016
2018
2020

Each year, the US government spends about a trillion dollars on defense, which is more than the following ten countries combined. However, many of our defense systems are antiquated and not even functional. For example, hundreds, if not thousands, of Air Force pilots are flying planes built before their birth, many of which are not even fly-worthy.

"The queen of the American fleet, and the centerpiece of the most powerful Navy the world has ever seen, the aircraft carrier, is in danger of becoming like the battleships it was originally designed to support:

big, expensive [>$10B], vulnerable

– and surprisingly irrelevant to the conflicts of the time.

....

It takes nearly 6,700 men and women to crew them, it costs about $6.5 million per day to operate each strike group."

— CAPT Henry J. Hendrix, USN (Ph.D.), March 2013 —

Alternatively, China spends its precious dollars on sophisticated hypersonic missiles that make the US's fancy toys defenseless. The Chinese DF-26 ballistic missiles that cost only a hundred thousand dollars can sink the "sitting ducks" of the US that cost north of $10 billion.

The US is acting irrationally, mirroring the Soviet Union with its doomsday doctrine driven by a few influential special interest groups from the $2 trillion industry and orthodox Bedouin sects[68]. US Defense spending may not have a basis on a rational strategy that is best for US citizens. Instead, many may be the result of lobbying by defense contractors. These contractors influence the congressmen by allocating the manufacturing plants and bases in their districts (thus influencing the employment). The Chinese may well be laughing at us as we drink from this poisoned financial chalice of prodigal spending filled with borrowed money from them. That also has been weaponized in their name (as enemy #1) but will never be used against them. Chinese quasi-institutional investors are significant contributors to many investment vehicles, including private equity firms, which own defense contractors. Ironically, some of the not so friendly Sovereign Wealth funds own at least some of our primary defense contractors too[69].

"When we hang the capitalists they will sell us the rope we use. "

Joseph Stalin

Like the Soviets witnessed the end of their empire by unilaterally entangling themselves in unnecessary political conflicts, we are also spilling our precious blood and treasure. Ironically, we are the copycats, making the same mistakes as the Russians in Afghanistan. It is impossible to conquer the Afghans; the Persians, Alexander the Great, Genghis Khan, Britain, and Russians failed. More recently, in the war-torn deserts of the Middle East, we smoked $5 trillion by getting involved in the tribal Bedouin wars.

This irrational exuberant adventurism is a gift to China. China is strategically focused, and they grew most spectacularly over our declining years, inspired by our stupidity. Since the US exports oil, there are no strategic values found in the Middle East other than the loss of precious blood and treasure. In summary, we are protecting the oil supplies to China, like what happened in Afghanistan and Pakistan, by helping China win their commercial interests.

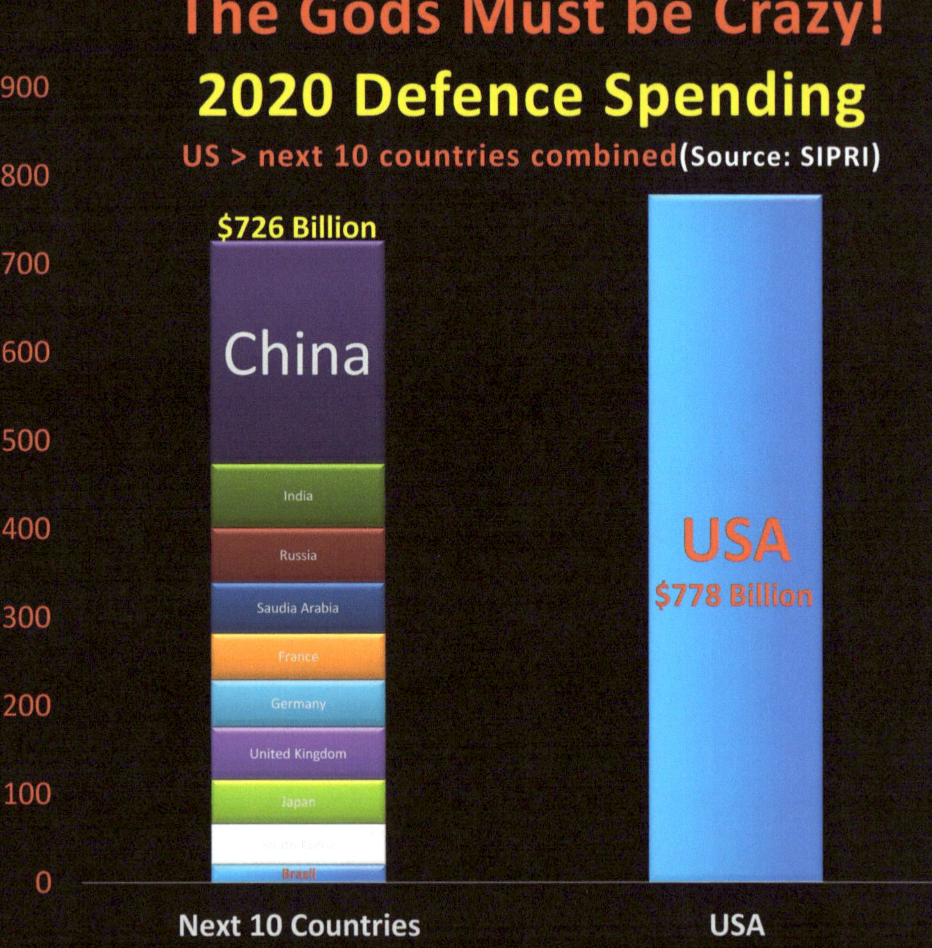

Meanwhile, China is rational and acting wisely as America once did in the Roosevelt (or even the Cold War) days, marshaling global alliances. There are no lobbyists in China, and they make rational decisions for their long-term security and commercial interests.

We should completely modernize the military for tomorrow's wars, not the prehistoric conventional warfare of the past, with public-private partnerships just as Franklin Roosevelt did. We need to have visionaries like

FDR to prepare for and win the third world war, which is now brewing, as FDR did in 1942 when his vision won the Second World War.

If we are not strategic and wise, we will not stand against the modern Chinese defense establishments. The chart below shows that the US is barely spending any money on the futuristic R&D necessary to survive the dragon. If we are not careful and strategic, our hawkish military adventurism and exceptionalism will humiliate us in the Middle Kingdoms' backyard. Sad to say, we are fighting tomorrow's wars with yesterday's strategy and weapons.

★ ★

The Gods Must be Crazy!
2020 US Defense Spending
Catacomb of Capitalism: Little R&D?

Source: OMB (Office of Management and Budget)

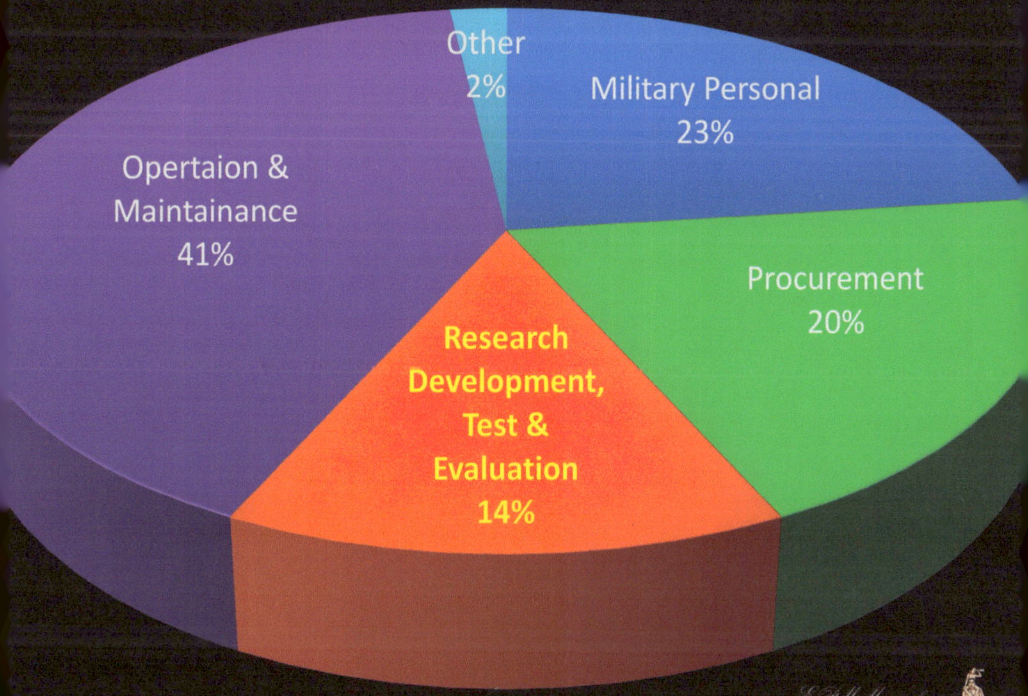

12. Digital Strategies and the Transformative Roadmap:

"To succeed, we need to imbibe the spirit of a comprehensive grand strategy."

Grand Strategy includes an indulgence of the power of norms (moral rightfulness), heaven, earth (physical environments), leadership, and finally, method and discipline (assessment of military capability, relative power potential).

Once all elements come together, a state can benefit from a grand strategy for success.

Adapted from Sun Tzu's The Art of War (476–221 BC)

During Roosevelt's first 100 days in office, he created the alphabet agencies, also known as the 'New Deal' agencies. At least 69 offices were created during Roosevelt's many terms as part of the "New Deal." There are three branches of government, and the executive branch controls most of the federal agencies. Under the executive branch, there are 15 executive departments and about 254 sub-agencies. Congress also established about 67 independent agencies and more than a dozen smaller boards, commissions, and committees.

The tree rots from the roots. Corrupt termites now infest most of those branches of the U.S. Government and the underlying agencies of the 19th century. Analyst James A. Thurber estimated that the number of working lobbyists was close to 100,000 and that this corrupt industry was bringing in $9 billion annually[70]. That is more than the GDP (2018) of over 50 countries under the United Nations flag. Recently, lobbying activity has increased and "going underground" as lobbyists use "increasingly sophisticated strategies" to obscure their activities. Even justice is also for sale through the millions of dark money campaign contributions[71]. The January 2010 Supreme Court Citizens United ruling unleashed a colossal wave of campaign spending that was extraordinarily unethical and corrupt by any judicious standard. Wall Street spent a record $2 billion trying to influence the 2016 presidential election in the United States. Lobbying is a fancy legal form of bribery or extortion, and in any other part of the world, it is called corruption.

★★★★★★★★★★★★★★★★★★★★★★★★★★

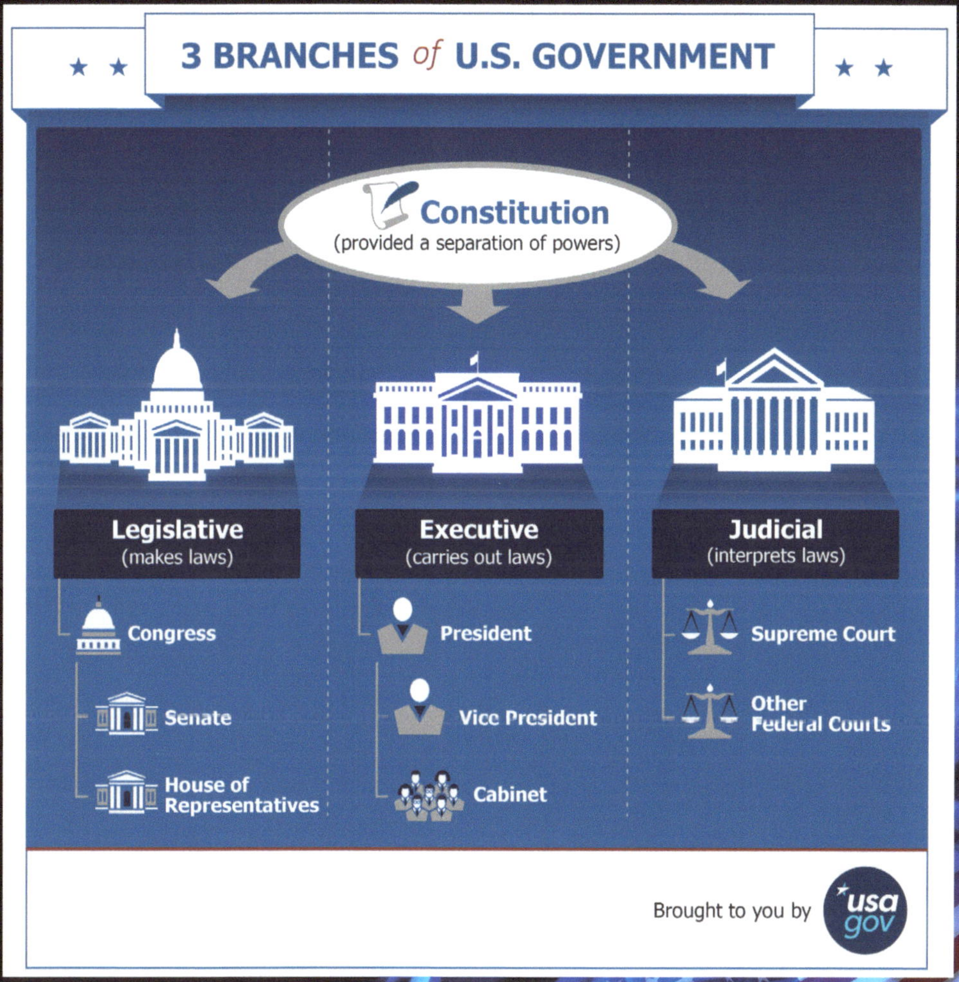

The current bureaucratic system has always served its purpose, especially a century ago under the well-intentioned Roosevelts. Unfortunately, many well-meaning organizations have become deep state frogs in the snake oil[72] swamp of Washington, D.C. What are our strategies and policies, given that recent geopolitical and economic disasters fundamentally weakened many of these systems? Do we have a vision and strategic roadmap to face this changing world order? We live in a new multi-dimensional era where many past arcane regulations need to transform into a 22nd-century digital world order.

"If your enemy is secure at all points, be prepared for him. If he is in superior strength, evade him. If your opponent is temperamental, seek to irritate him. Pretend to be weak, that he may grow arrogant. If he is taking his ease, give him no rest. If his forces are united, separate them. Attack him where he is unprepared, appear where you are not expected."

Sun Tzu's The Art of War (476–221 BC)

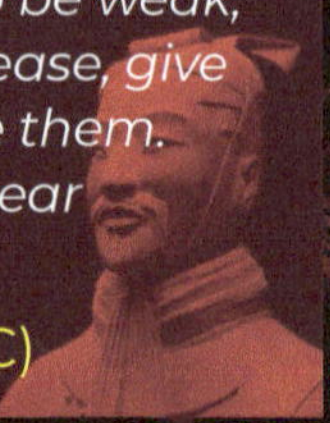

China is the only resilient ancient civilization to fall four times and bounce back each time. Since the imperial decline of the First Opium War (1839 to 1842) and the humiliation that came with it, every Chinese leader has sought to recapture lost glories at home and abroad. The vision of the Chinese Communist Party (CCP) is no secret: Xi Jinping is determined to make The Middle Kingdom great again. The CCP is utilizing "geo-technological" strategies and policies. China leads the way to Global Primacy through the multi-trillion-dollar New Silk Road (Belt and Road Initiative (BRI)) and Digital Silk Road (DSR), intent on colonizing Asia, the Middle East, Africa, and Europe. Structuring a comprehensive trade infrastructure for Chinese products, BRI offers China's long-term strategic shift around advanced technologies and military interests. These elements include 5G telecommunications, robotics, artificial intelligence (AI), and maritime engineering for defense interests.

Instead of extreme Financial Engineering tactics, we need to focus on long-term Value Engineering strategies. Value Engineering should be the aspiration for a "shining city upon a hill." Financial wealth is just a by-product. My generation has failed the youth. They are ill-prepared for the digital era and grossly lacking in STEM capabilities. We need to abandon the ostrich syndrome of burying our heads in the sand and recognize the changing dynamics of the global world order. If we do not, digital dragons like Huawei, Alibaba, Tencent, and Baidu will shape the world. China will make sure that these dragons leave their footprint in countries economically colonized by the Middle Kingdom.

In today's populist environment, it will be challenging for the US to find leaders like the Roosevelts who might reverse its decline. I hope it will be less traumatic, whereby we accept the realities as gracefully, as the British did when they passed the baton to us, rather than slipping into obscurity.

"Steve Hilton: A lot of people say that China wants to replace the US as the superpower..., Do you believe that that's their intention?" Trump: "Yes, I do. Why wouldn't it be? They're very ambitious people. They're very smart. They're great people. It's a great culture."

Fox News interview (05-19-19)

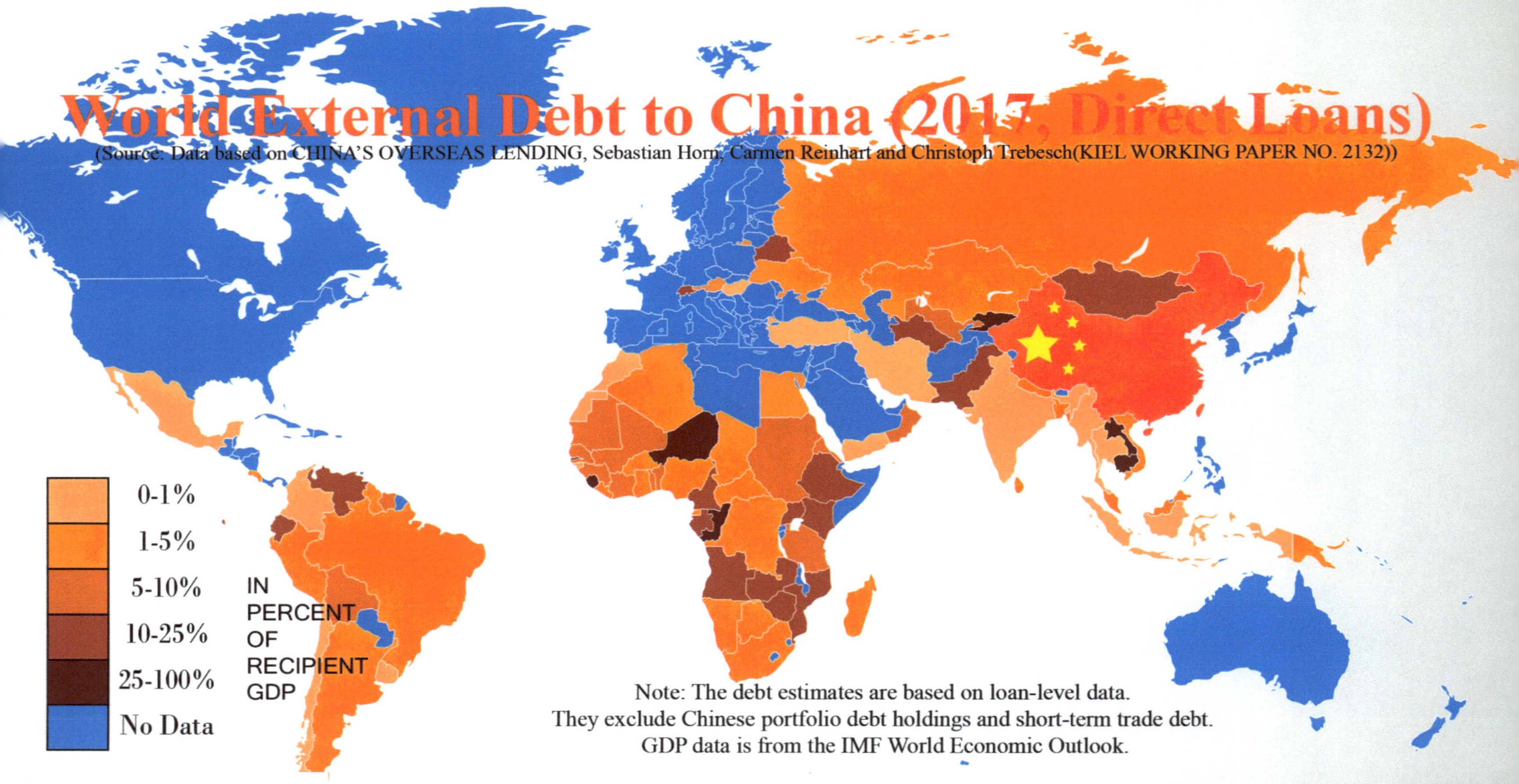
World External Debt to China (2017, Direct Loans)
(Source: Data based on CHINA'S OVERSEAS LENDING, Sebastian Horn, Carmen Reinhart and Christoph Trebesch(KIEL WORKING PAPER NO. 2132))
0-1%
1-5%
5-10%
10-25%
25-100%
No Data
IN PERCENT OF RECIPIENT GDP
Note: The debt estimates are based on loan-level data.
They exclude Chinese portfolio debt holdings and short-term trade debt.
GDP data is from the IMF World Economic Outlook.

EPILOGUE

The hand has become dealt with, and if we fail to play our trump card soon, China will send its mercenaries to collect the tolls from the US and the close to 100 countries it has economically and digitally colonized since the financial tsunami of 2008.

COVID-19 has exposed our deficiencies; even under the Presidential Defense Production Act, we are held hostage to China for our 3M-made facemasks and necessary personal protective equipment (PPE).

The US Economy that Roosevelt built was around 40% (in 1960) of the World's GDP (Gross Domestic Product). It has fallen to less than 15% in PPP, whereas China rapidly increases its share beyond 20%. Thanks to its reserve status, 79.5% of all world trade is still conducted in US dollars. With our extreme financial engineering, we have squandered our goodwill. If we do not get our act together, and quickly, our empire and enterprise days will become endangered.

"The highest excellence is winning without fighting, not decimating every adversary you encounter. Since destruction clearly isn't your goal and victory is, leaving things intact maximizes your gains and helps you to mend your fences with your adversary."

Sun Tzu's The Art of War (476–221 BC)

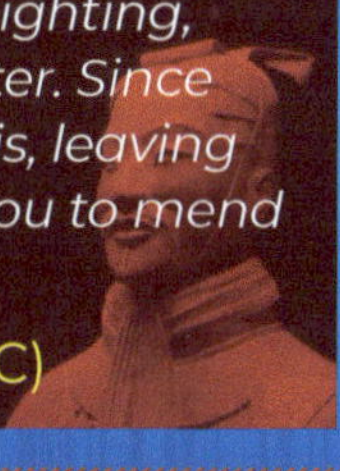

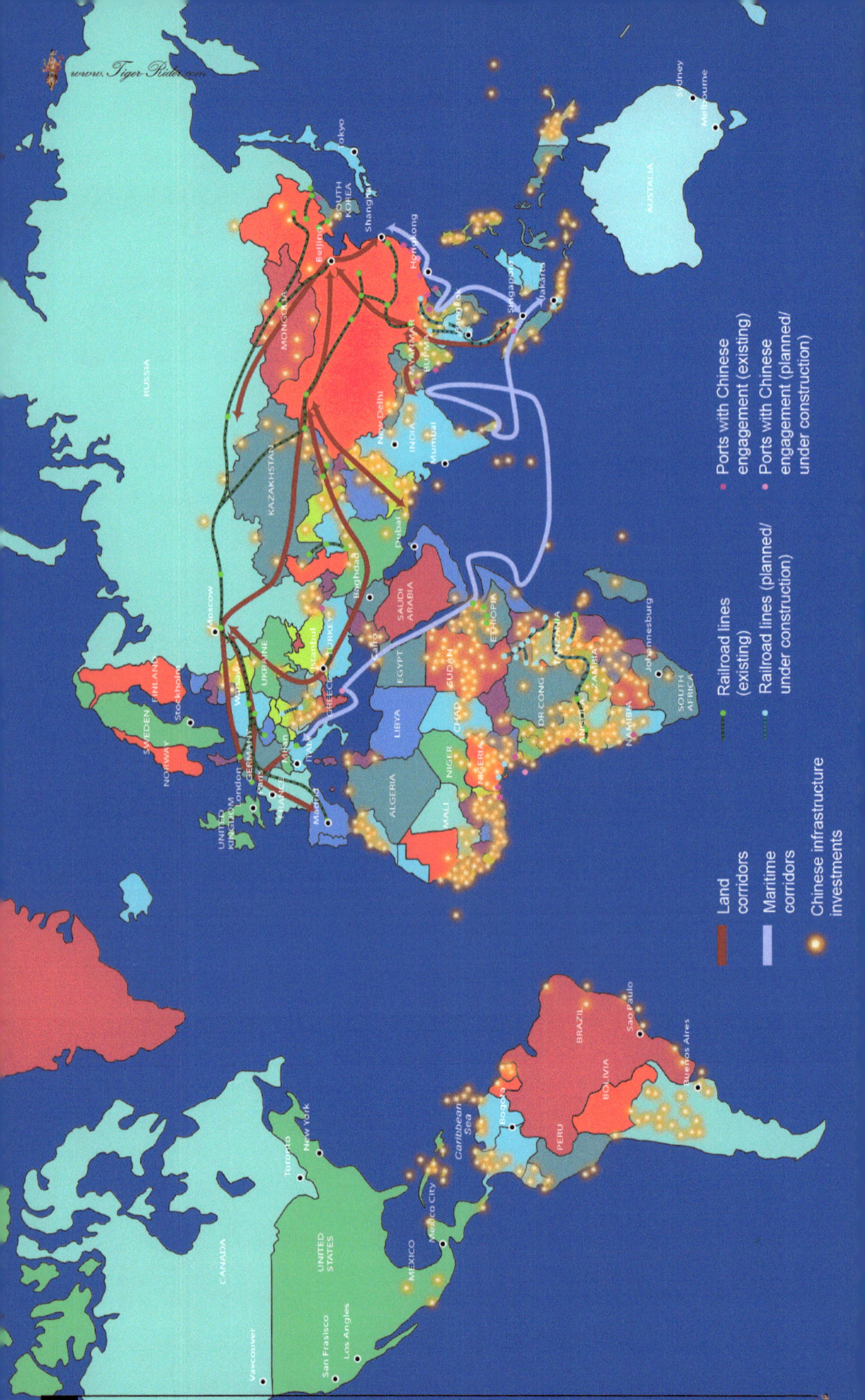
Land corridors
Maritime corridors
Chinese infrastructure investments
Railroad lines (existing)
Railroad lines (planned/ under construction)
Ports with Chinese engagement (existing)
Ports with Chinese engagement (planned/ under construction)
RUSSIA
MONGOLIA
KAZAKHSTAN
Beijing
SOUTH KOREA
Tokyo
Shanghai
Hong Kong
Bangkok
Singapore
Jakarta
MYANMAR
BURMA
New Delhi
INDIA
Mumbai
Dubai
Baghdad
SAUDI ARABIA
TURKEY
Istanbul
Moscow
UKRAINE
FINLAND
Stockholm
SWEDEN
NORWAY
Warsaw
GERMANY
London
UNITED KINGDOM
Paris
FRANCE
Madrid
Milan
ITALY
GREECE
Cairo
EGYPT
LIBYA
ALGERIA
MALI
NIGER
NIGERIA
CHAD
SUDAN
ETHIOPIA
DR CONGO
ANGOLA
ZAMBIA
NAMIBIA
SOUTH AFRICA
Johannesburg
AUSTALIA
Sydney
Melbourne
CANADA
UNITED STATES
Vavcouver
San Frasisco
Los Angles
Toronto
New York
MEXICO
Mexico City
Caribbean Sea
Bogota
PERU
BRAZIL
BOLIVIA
Sao Paulo
Buenos Aires

Now is not the time to build a wall around our ivory tower and risk entrapment in foreclosure hell. No single autocratic person can address the multi-dimensional challenges and exponential downward spiral resulting from black swans in the "New Normal." Rather than unilateralism, the time has come to refine our soft skills, reach out to the rest of the 96% of humanity, and re-architect our Noah's Enterprise Ark as the Roosevelts did when they led us down the path to becoming a superpower a century ago.

If we fail in this, some extreme left populists will resort to communism (the more or less equal redistribution of wealth), and most from the right will become fascist militia (autocratic state-controlled capitalism). The survival of American enterprise has become intertwined with the rise and fall of its sponsoring godfather, the US empire. We have witnessed this in the past four centuries with the largest enterprises, such as the Dutch (~$10T) and British (~$5T) East India companies. Unfortunately, many enterprise dinosaurs who practice extreme financial engineering will fall victim to intellectual property vultures (mostly from China).

We need to learn from the Roosevelts, who architected our great capitalistic foundation that has lasted three-fourths of a century. We lead the coalition to establish new "Marshall Plans" to save the countries that China has economically and digitally colonized before it is too late.

The foundational architecture should have the basis on:

1. Leadership
2. Science, Technology, Engineering, and Mathematics (STEM) Education
3. Research and Strategic Technology
4. Infrastructure Architecture
5. Digital Architecture
6. Knowledge Management
7. Diplomacy
8. World Currency Gold Standard
9. Electro-Dollar
10. Financial Capital
11. Security
12. Transformative Digital Grand Strategies and Regulations

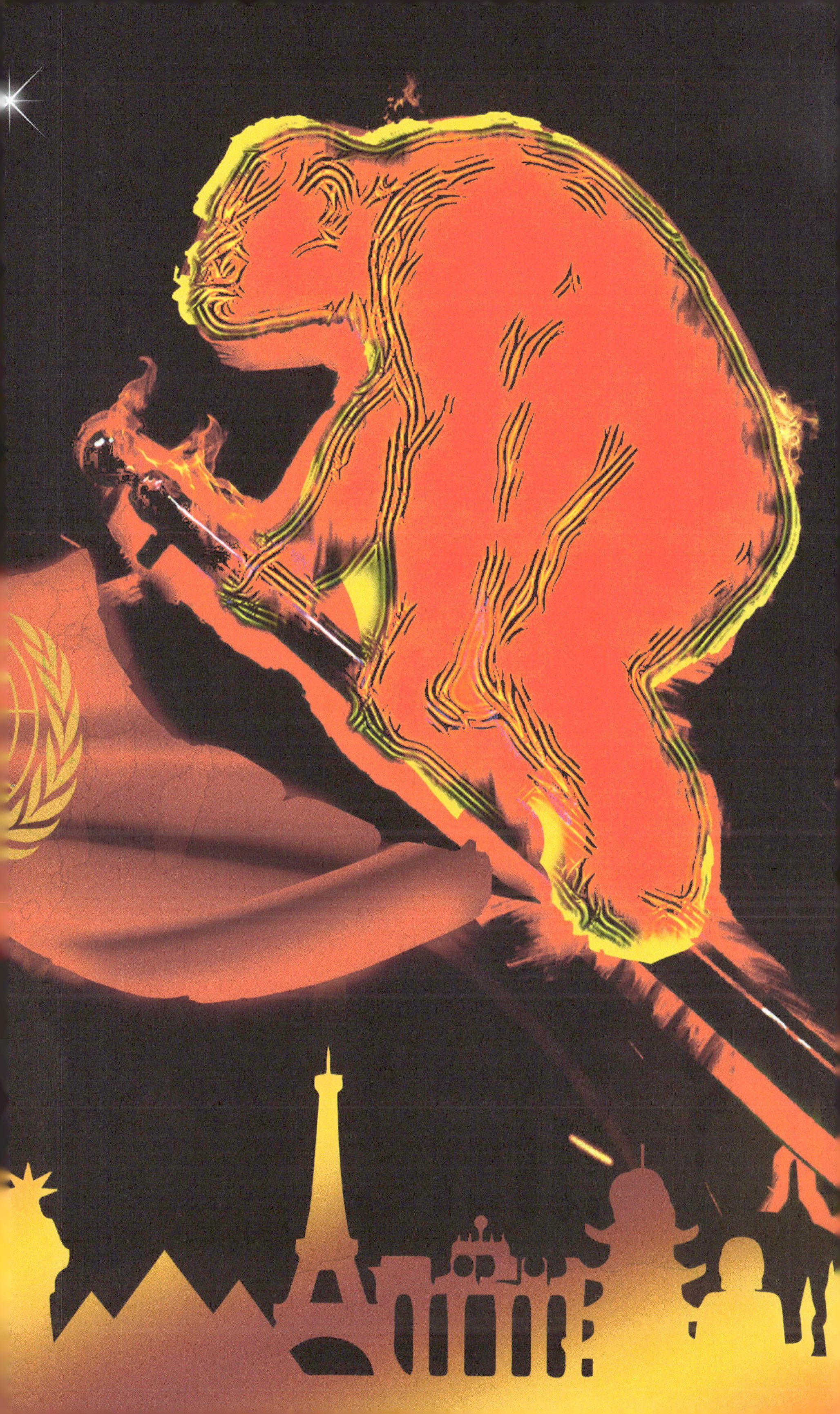

I am a contrarian who predicted the 2008 economic tsunami, which was relatively easy given that it was mostly US-centric. This time, the situation is much more voracious and multi-dimensional with COVID-19 and civil unrest acting as black swan global generational tectonic shifts. I hope I am wrong in my analysis this time. I am passing this research and analysis to you to challenge my unique perspective and to stress-test it.

Thus far, the US has given incredible gifts to the Middle Kingdom through our extreme financial engineering and choking the golden goose (betraying their profitable enterprises for a few selfish dollar bonuses). If we do not plan the **22nd Century Digital Age New Normal Noah's Enterprise Ark**, I foresee a future that mimics the Fourth Reich[73], serving as slaves for *The Man in The High Castle*[74], reminiscent of the Netflix Documentary *American Factory*[75].

Yeah! It's halftime, America![76]

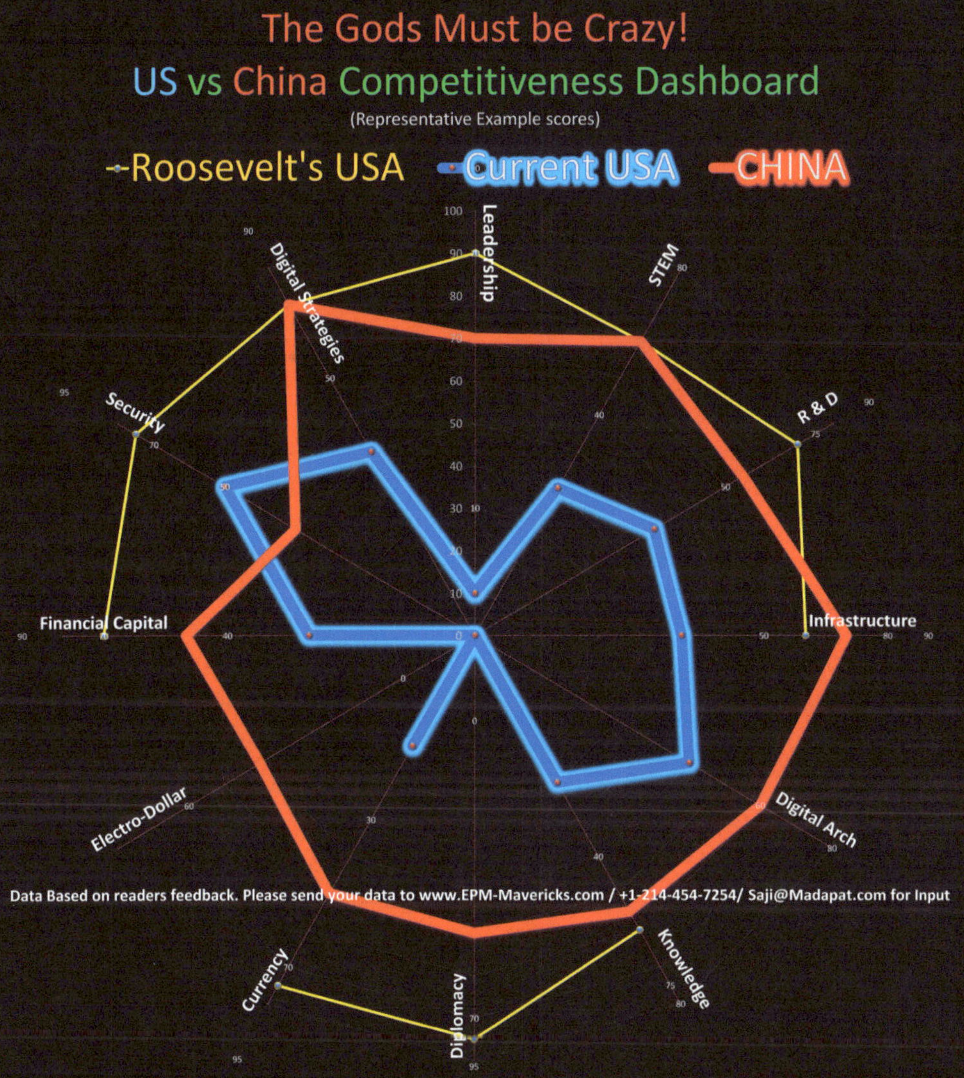
The Gods Must be Crazy!
US vs China Competitiveness Dashboard
(Representative Example scores)
Roosevelt's USA
Current USA
CHINA
Leadership
STEM
R & D
Infrastructure
Digital Arch
Knowledge
Diplomacy
Currency
Electro-Dollar
Financial Capital
Security
Digital Strategies
Data Based on readers feedback. Please send your data to www.EPM-Mavericks.com / +1-214-454-7254/ Saji@Madapat.com for Input

YEAH! IT'S HALFTIME, AMERICA!

Ay Yi Yai Yi! We are in the middle of The New World Order!

ABOUT THE AUTHOR

A BRIEF HISTORY OF MY NOMADIC RE-INCARNATIONS

★ ★

"To fight and conquer in all our battles is not supreme excellence; supreme excellence consists in breaking the enemy's resistance without fighting."

Sun Tzu's The Art of War (476–221 BC)

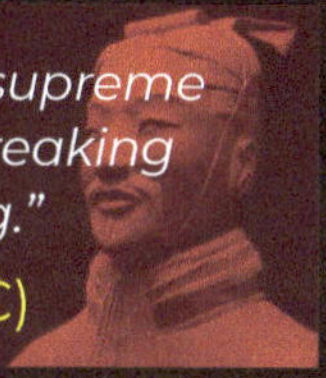

I was born and raised in God's Own Country, Kerala, a tropical paradise in India. In Kerala, we are followers of St. Thomas, the Apostle, educated by Christian missionaries brought by colonizers from Portugal, France, and Britain. 100% literacy and high educational standards in Kerala have led to many progressive movements, including Communism. Kerala has many unique records, such as a model COVID-19 recovery rate that is higher than most Western countries. Kerala is the first-place communists became democratically elected to power in world history and have ruled since 1957. The resulting industrial desert brought on by Communism forced me to pack up my bags after obtaining my Industrial Engineering degree (with specialization in Total Quality Management) and seek a job in Bombay (the commercial capital of India, now called Mumbai).

I soon realized my prospects beyond the factory floor were limited by my dark skin (as a lungi-wearing Kala Madrasi). Fearing for my future, I fled to the South to escape the racist professional ladder. I obtained my MBA in finance as a candidate for national integration. Providentially for me, in 1990, the entire Indian economy collapsed under the weight of the half-a-century-old mighty Indian License Raj. The result was a liberalized Indian economy. The timing was impeccable, as it provided me the opportunity to start my career as an Investment Banking Analyst. Fortune smiled upon me again when India's 1996 stock market crash allowed me to come out of my investment banking career.

India took the socialist route and, during the conflict of the 1970s with Pakistan, it declared emergency rule. Due to the Pakistan war and other non-alignments, the US and India's relationship soured, and IBM abandoned India. Hail to the vacuum (to be filled), TCS and other Indian IT conglomerates were born out of desperation. They coded us in IT to kick-start the legacy computers and mainframes left behind by IBM. Thanks to the biggest blunder in business history (Y2K), IBM and the other western enterprises saw us ('*Cyber Coolies*') as the thrifty solution to fix the doomsday Armageddon code.

During this time, I managed to migrate from corporate finance to ERP (Enterprise Resource Planning) solutions and snatched my passport to the epitome of capitalism, the USA. Nevertheless, in 2000, the (Netherlands-based) BaaN Brothers got involved in the Dutch scandal, and the #3 ERP (BaaN) system I was riding became a dead horse.

Since then, I have spent over a decade volunteering for PMI. I have etched my name on PMI's key standards (including PMBOK, OPM3, PP&PM, etc.), thanks to my PMI papers, publications, and books (especially Project Portfolio Management Standard). I even served on Gartner's PPM board room panel. I later became one of the three PM Methodology SMEs at E&Y. In 2008, amid the economic tsunami, I served as an advisor to the CFO office, setting up the Project Portfolio Management Office for

a Fortune 10 World's Most Admired Company. I saved them around half a billion dollars, but I became the victim of my short-term financial engineering. I managed to capitalize on the 90s legacy Hyperion Enterprise and moved on to the fancy world of a CFO's suite of products for more prominent Financial Engineering in the BIG4 consulting world.

In 2009, I packed my bags for the Cambodian Jungles in search of answers from the bottom of the pyramid through Chinese GIFT (Global Institute for Tomorrow)[77] – a Clinton Global Young Executive Leadership Program (YLP). The more I examined the finance world in the West, the more disillusioned I became. I lost faith in the rollercoasters of flash markets. 90% of today's stock market without long-term fundamental values is chasing stock buybacks, the Tweets, QE[78], the hot dollars, and high-frequency algorithmic flash gambles by BOTs. Hail to Hernando de Soto, I was born again to The Mystery of Capital Gospel. Since 9/11, I have won a few dollars betting against the conventional Western market wisdom by gambling in Petro China[79] and Total[80].

After returning from the wilderness of the Cambodian killing fields[81], I reincarnated my career yet again, becoming an EPM (Enterprise Performance Management) consultant out of the 2008 Economic Tsunami in the BIG4 world. I made 95% of my net worth between 2008 and 2011 by betting against conventional wisdom. When the whole world deleveraged, I leveraged to the extreme in some of the most iconic real estate in the world, which was on Fire-Sale. I do have a fair share of blood on my hands with mindless EPM Financial Engineering through fancy jargon (aka Cost Cutting) such as Tax Effective Supply Chain Management (TE-SCM), Business/Finance/IT Transformation, BPR, Six Sigma and Pricing and Profitability strategy.

To greenwash my guilt, I had the fantastic honor of volunteering for the most extensive Professional Not-for-Profit for over a decade (PMI [Project Management Institute]), serving ~3 million professionals, including over 500,000 members in 208 countries around the world. I have contributed to about half a dozen books and ~50 publications/presentations. I became involved in several Entrepreneur of the Year (EOY) Awards at Ernst & Young.

Sadly, after over two decades, it looks like I need to ride back through that Mad Max fury redemption road and climb through the apocalypse rubble of Roosevelt's capitalist nostalgic era.

Thris
The Festival of Festiv

HUMBLE REQUEST TO REVIEW MY BOOK

★★★★★★★★★★★★★★★★★★★★★★★★★

I trust that you enjoyed reading this book. I'd like to hear from you and humbly request that you to take a few minutes to post a review on Amazon. Your feedback and support will significantly improve my writing craft for future books and make this book even more commendable. This is a living manuscript and will continuously evolve based on your constructive wisdom (***direct contact details*** @ www.Epm-Mavericks.com). Thank you in advance!

Acronyms

- ★ Intellectual property (IP)
- ★ Belt and Road Initiative (BRI)
- ★ Digital Silk Road (DSR)
- ★ Internet of Things (IoT)
- ★ The Middle Kingdom (China)
- ★ One Belt, One Road (OBOR)
- ★ Asian Infrastructure Investment Bank (AIIB)
- ★ Purchasing Power Parity (PPP)
- ★ Gross domestic product (GDP)
- ★ Black Lives Matter (BLM)
- ★ George Floyd riots (FLOYD)
- ★ Political Action Committee (PAC)
- ★ Swamp (Washington DC)
- ★ Mergers and Acquisitions (M&A)
- ★ Facebook, Amazon, Apple, Netflix, and Google (FAANG)
- ★ Global Institute for Tomorrow (GIFT - https://global-inst.com/learn/)
- ★ Science, Technology, Engineering, and Mathematics (STEM)
- ★ Tax Effective Supply Chain Management (TESCM)
- ★ Robotic Automation in Cloud (BOTs)
- ★ Business Process Outsourcing (BPO)
- ★ Chinese Communist Party (CCP)
- ★ Franklin D. Roosevelt (FDR)
- ★ Theodore Roosevelt (TR)
- ★ Organization for Economic Cooperation and Development (OECD)
- ★ Artificial Intelligence (AI)
- ★ The Trans-Pacific Partnership (TPP)
- ★ Society for Worldwide Interbank Financial Telecommunication (SWIFT)
- ★ Special-Purpose Vehicle (SPV)
- ★ Blockchain Service Network (BSN)
- ★ New Development Bank (NDB)
- ★ Cross-Border Interbank Payment System (CIPS)

Art Images Used in This Book

Theyyam, the 'Dance of Gods': The blissful state of Kerala has a greater wealth of cultural traditions than any other part of the world. Theyyam is the 'Dance of Gods.' The flamboyant dance incorporates elements and rituals from the prehistoric ages. There are about 456 types of Theyyam (theyyakkolams) and performed in the North Malabar region of India, which is my home region. https://www.tiger-rider.com/Client-Galleries/Rhodes/

https://en.wikipedia.org/wiki/Theyyam

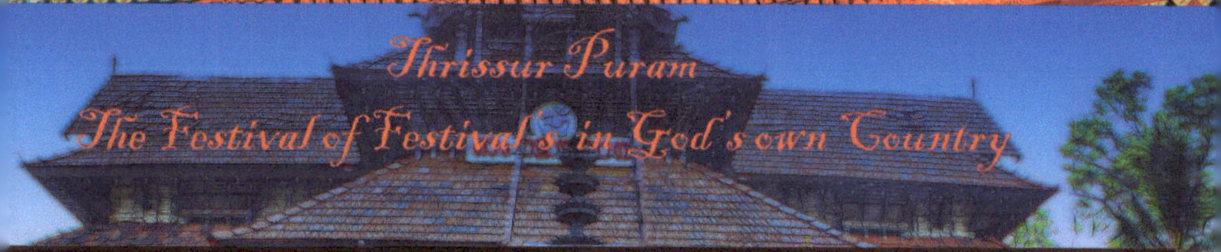

Thrissur Puram
The Festival of Festival's in God's own Country

Thrissur Puram, the Festival of Festivals: Thrissur (cultural capital of India) is my hometown in India – That is where I spend 4 Puram's while I was doing my Engineering. I always dreamed about watching Puram closely – but that used to be an impossible dream among the Lakhs of attendees every year. Finally, I was granted once in a lifetime Devine access at Rostrum at Divine Durbar (guest pass issued by Trichur collector), unfretted access (media pass) to everything by both Thiruvambadi & Parammekkavu Devaswom. https://www.tiger-rider.com/Client-Galleries/Puram/ http://en.wikipedia.org/wiki/Thrissur_Pooram

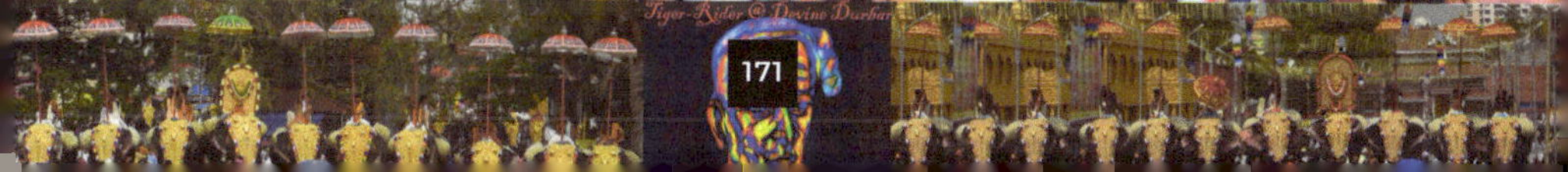

Kathakali, the Art of Story Telling: Kathakali (Malayalam: കഥകളി) is a major form of classical Indian dance. It is a "story play" genre of art, but one distinguished by the elaborately colorful make-up, costumes, and face masks that the traditionally male actor-dancers wear. Kathakali is a Hindu performance art in the Malayalam-speaking southwestern region of India (Kerala). https://www.tiger-rider.com/Client-Galleries/KathakaliICCT/ https://en.wikipedia.org/wiki/Kathakali

ENDNOTES

1 Chiraq is a nickname for Chicago, Illinois. It combines the words Chicago with Iraq and is used to refer to certain violent areas in Chicago, likening them to a warzone. https://www.dictionary.com/e/slang/chiraq/#:~:text=Chiraq%20is%20a%20nickname%20for,likening%20them%20to%20a%20warzone

2 In political science, the term banana republic describes a politically unstable country with an economy dependent upon the exportation of a limited-resource product, such as bananas or minerals. https://www.theatlantic.com/politics/archive/2013/01/is-the-us-on-the-verge-of-becoming-a-banana-republic/267048/

3 Boarding up is the process of installing boards on the windows and doors of a property to protect it from storm damage, to protect unused, vacant, or abandoned property, and/or to prevent unauthorized access by squatters, looters, or vandals. https://www.wbez.org/stories/protest-art-has-covered-boarded-up-businesses-will-it-be-preserved/e3db8017-a6ba-4dde-9bc3-3d17f6ee5392

4 Throughout the last 5000 years, China has been known by many different names but the most traditional name that China has used to refer to itself is Zhonggou which means Middle Kingdom (or sometimes translated as Central Kingdom). http://www.learnmartialartsinchina.com/kung-fu-school-blog/why-is-china-called-the-middle-kingdom/#:~:text=Throughout%20the%20last%205000%20years,sometimes%20translated%20as%20Central%20Kingdom)

5 https://www.britannica.com/place/Third-Reich

6 Dutch East India Company, by name of United East India Company, Dutch Vereenigde Oost-Indische Compagnie, is a trading company founded in the Dutch Republic (present-day Netherlands) in 1602 to protect that state's trade in the Indian Ocean and to assist in the Dutch war of independence from Spain. https://www.pbs.org/wgbh/roadshow/stories/articles/2013/1/7/dutch-east-india-company-worlds-first-multinational/

7 The East India Company was an English company formed for the exploitation of trade with East and Southeast Asia and India. Incorporated by royal charter on December 31, 1600, it was started as a monopolistic trading body so that England could participate in the East Indian spice trade. https://www.bbc.co.uk/programmes/n3csxl34

8 The New Deal was a series of programs, public work projects, financial reforms, and regulations enacted by President Franklin D. Roosevelt in the United States between 1933 and 1939. It responded to needs for relief, reform, and recovery from the Great Depression. https://www.fdrlibrary.org/great-depression-new-deal

9 https://www.npr.org/sections/codeswitch/2013/08/26/215761377/a-history-of-snake-oil-salesmen

10 The 2008 global financial crisis sits among the most prevalent recent examples of an economic tsunami. The subprime mortgage market in the U.S. acted as a trigger in this case, with large investment banks (IBs) miscalculating the amount of risk in certain collateralized debt instruments. https://www.investopedia.com/terms/e/economictsunami.asp#:~:text=The%202008%20global%20financial%20crisis,in%20certain%20collateralized%20debt%20instruments.

11 Debt-trap diplomacy describes diplomacy based on debt carried out in the bilateral relations between countries with an often-alleged negative intent. Although the term has been applied to the lending practices of many countries and the International Monetary Fund, it is currently most commonly associated with the People's Republic of China. https://foreignpolicy.com/2020/03/23/china-coronavirus-belt-and-road-bri-boost-debt-diplomacy/

12 The Belt and Road Initiative, formerly known as One Belt One Road or OBOR for short, is a global infrastructure development strategy adopted by the Chinese government in 2013 to invest in various countries and international organizations. https://www.oecd.org/finance/Chinas-Belt-and-Road-Initiative-in-the-global-trade-investment-and-finance-landscape.pdf

13 The Marshall Plan (officially the European Recovery Program, ERP) was an American initiative passed in 1948 for foreign aid to Western Europe. https://history.state.gov/milestones/1945-1952/marshall-plan

14 The "Digital Silk Road" (DSR) was introduced in 2015 by an official Chinese government white paper, as a component of Beijing's Belt and Road Initiative (BRI). For years, it has been less an identifiable set of projects as much as it was a brand for virtually any telecommunications or data-related business operations or product sales by China-based tech firms in Africa, Asia, Europe, Latin America, or the Caribbean — home to the 100+ "BRI countries." https://carnegieendowment.org/2020/05/08/will-china-control-global-internet-via-its-digital-silk-road-pub-81857

15 The Thousand Talents Plan (TTP) (Chinese: 千人计划; pinyin: Qiān rén jìhuà) or Thousand Talents Program (Chinese: 海外高层次人才引进计划; pinyin: Hǎiwài gāo céngcì réncái yǐnjìn jìhuà) was established in 2008 by the central government of China to recognize and recruit leading international experts in scientific research, innovation, and entrepreneurship. https://www.hsgac.senate.gov/imo/media/doc/2019-11-18%20PSI%20Staff%20Report%20-%20China's%20Talent%20Recruitment%20Plans.pdf

16 An expatriate (often shortened to expat) is a person residing in a country other than their native country. https://www.merriam-webster.com/dictionary/expatriate

17 https://itif.org/publications/2020/06/22/new-report-shows-unfair-chinese-government-support-huawei-and-zte-has-harmed

18 In Russian culture, kompromat, short for "compromising material", is damaging information about a politician, a businessperson, or other public figures, used to create negative publicity, as well as for blackmail and extortion. https://www.newyorker.com/news/swamp-chronicles/a-theory-of-trump-kompromat

19 Having set up beachheads in Asia, Europe, and Africa, China's AI companies are now pushing into Latin America, a region the Chinese government describes as a "core economic interest." Venezuela recently debuted a new national ID-card system that logs citizens' political affiliations in a database built by ZTE. In a grim irony, for years Chinese companies hawked many of these surveillance products at a security expo in Xinjiang, the home province of the Uighurs. https://www.theatlantic.com/magazine/archive/2020/09/china-ai-surveillance/614197/

20 https://www.theatlantic.com/magazine/archive/2020/09/china-ai-surveillance/614197/

21 https://www.brookings.edu/opinions/the-aiib-and-the-one-belt-one-road/

22 https://en.wikipedia.org/wiki/List_of_countries_by_GDP_(PPP)

23 https://www.heritage.org/defense/commentary/chinas-defense-spending-larger-it-looks

24 https://youtu.be/2J9y6s_ukBQ

25 https://www.nytimes.com/2018/01/18/us/politics/trump-border-wall-immigration.html

26 https://fee.org/articles/the-medical-cartel-is-keeping-health-care-costs-high/#:~:text=Though%20few%20Americans%20realize%20it%2C%20health%20care%20is%20a%20monopoly.,-Cartels%20Protecting%20Doctors&text=Cartels%20Protecting%20Doctors-,Both%20directly%20or%20indirectly%2C%20the%20AMA%20also%20controls%20the%20prices,payment%20policies%20of%20insurance%20companies.

27 https://www.oecd-ilibrary.org/education/education-at-a-glance-2018_eag-2018-en

28 https://educationdata.org/international-student-enrollment-statistics/

29 https://www.oecd.org/pisa/pisa-2015-results-in-focus.pdf

30 https://www.sentencingproject.org/wp-content/uploads/2015/11/Americans-with-Criminal-Records-Poverty-and-Opportunity-Profile.pdf

31 https://www.brennancenter.org/our-work/research-reports/citizens-united-explained

32 https://www.marketwatch.com/story/airlines-and-boeing-want-a-bailout-but-look-how-much-theyve-spent-on-stock-buybacks-2020-03-18

33 https://www.marketwatch.com/story/airlines-and-boeing-want-a-bailout-but-look-how-much-theyve-spent-on-stock-buybacks-2020-03-18

34 https://www.imf.org/external/pubs/ft/fandd/2019/09/tackling-global-tax-havens-shaxon.htm

35 The Indian version of feudalism. A zamindar, in the Indian subcontinent was an autonomous or semiautonomous ruler of a state who accepted the suzerainty of the Emperor of Hindustan. The term means landowner in Persian. Typically, hereditary, zamindars held enormous tracts of land and control over their peasants, from whom they reserved the right to collect tax on behalf of imperial courts or for military purposes. https://www.britannica.com/topic/zamindar

36 Gordon Gekko is a fictional character who appears as the villain in the popular 1987 Oliver Stone movie "Wall Street". https://review.chicagobooth.edu/behavioral-science/2017/article/moral-ambivalence-gordon-gekko

37 A dark science fiction thriller that's relevant to present-day society and existing social and economic inequality. https://www.sonypictures.com/movies/elysium

38 Quote from The Mystery of Capital: Why Capitalism Triumphs in the West and Fails Everywhere by Hernando De Soto (Author) https://www.amazon.com/dp/B06XCFW5ZN/

39 https://www.sba.gov/sites/default/files/FAQ_Sept_2012.pdf

40 A dark science fiction thriller that's relevant to present-day society and existing social and economic inequality. https://en.wikipedia.org/wiki/Elysium_(film)

41 https://www.cnn.com/2020/01/07/tech/boz-trump-facebook/index.html

42 https://www.swift.com/sites/default/files/documents/swift_bi_currency_evolution_infopaper_57128.pdf

43 https://www.thebalance.com/black-wednesday-george-soros-bet-against-britain-1978944

44 https://en.wikipedia.org/wiki/1997_Asian_financial_crisis#:~:text=Malaysian%20Prime%20Minister%20Mahathir%20Mohamad,sold%20it%20short%20in%201997.

45 https://www.rottentomatoes.com/tv/the_man_in_the_high_castle/s01

46 https://www.rottentomatoes.com/m/american_factory

47 https://en.wikipedia.org/wiki/Snake_oil

48 https://www.imf.org/en/Publications/GFSR/Issues/2019/10/01/global-financial-stability-report-october-2019

49 The namesake of this book comes from the 1980 Comedy film "The Gods Must Be Crazy," in which an empty Coca-Cola bottle is dropped from a plane onto a community of African bushmen. The bottle is a gift from the gods, but after it leads to in-fighting among the villagers, the tribal leaders decide to return it to the gods by having one of the villagers' journeys to the end of the world

to drop the bottle over the edge. Through my own metaphorical coke bottle, I can see the dawn of a new empire. This book serves as a testament to my views on restoring the current empire (capitalism and enterprises) before it is too late. https://www.rottentomatoes.com/m/the_gods_must_be_crazy

50 https://global-inst.com/

51 https://www.history.com/topics/cold-war/the-khmer-rouge

52 https://en.wikipedia.org/wiki/Snake_wine

53 https://www.cato.org/cato-journal/winter-2018/against-helicopter-money

54 https://www.investopedia.com/terms/g/gordon-gekko.asp

55 https://www.investopedia.com/terms/q/quantitative-easing.asp

56 https://youtu.be/8iXdsvgpwc8

57 "Triple talaq", as it's known, allows a husband to divorce his wife by repeating the word "talaq" (divorce) three times in any form, including email https://en.wikipedia.org/wiki/Divorce_in_Islam

58 https://en.wikipedia.org/wiki/List_of_countries_by_GDP_(PPP)

59 https://www.whitehouse.gov/presidential-actions/memorandum-order-defense-production-act-regarding-3m-company/

60 https://www.theatlantic.com/education/archive/2018/09/why-is-college-so-expensive-in-america/569884/

61 https://www.theregister.com/2021/08/20/china_5g_progress/

62 https://www.mckinsey.com/business-functions/organization/our-insights/getting-practical-about-the-future-of-work

63 https://www.swift.com/sites/default/files/documents/swift_bi_currency_evolution_infopaper_57128.pdf

64 https://data.worldbank.org/indicator/CM.MKT.LDOM.NO?end=2018&locations=US&start=1996

65 https://watson.brown.edu/costsofwar/papers/2021/ProfitsOfWar

66 Saudi Sovereign-Wealth Fund Buys Stakes in Facebook, Boeing, Cisco Systems - WSJ

67 https://www.whitehouse.gov/briefing-room/presidential-actions/2021/09/03/executive-order-on-declassification-review-of-certain-documents-concerning-the-terrorist-attacks-of-september-11-2001/

68 https://en.wikipedia.org/wiki/Charlie_Wilson%27s_War_(film), https://www.pbs.org/wgbh/frontline/film/bitter-rivals-iran-and-saudi-arabia/, https://en.wikipedia.org/wiki/Syriana, https://www.pbs.org/frontlineworld/stories/r4.html https://www.pbs.org/independentlens/films/shadow-world/

69 https://www.wsj.com/articles/saudi-sovereign-wealth-fund-buys-stakes-in-facebook-boeing-cisco-systems-11589633300

70 https://en.wikipedia.org/wiki/Lobbying_in_the_United_States
https://www.american.edu/spa/ccps/upload/thurber-testimony.pdf

71 https://www.brennancenter.org/our-work/analysis-opinion/how-campaign-spending-judicial-elections-subverts-justice

72 https://en.wikipedia.org/wiki/Snake_oil

73 https://www.britannica.com/place/Third-Reich

74 https://www.rottentomatoes.com/tv/the_man_in_the_high_castle/s01

75 https://www.rottentomatoes.com/m/american_factory

76 https://youtu.be/8iXdsvgpwc8

77 https://global-inst.com/

78 https://www.investopedia.com/terms/q/quantitative-easing.asp

79 http://www.petrochina.com.cn/ptr/index.shtml

80 https://www.total.com/

81 https://www.history.com/topics/cold-war/the-khmer-rouge

ACKNOWLEDGMENTS

I want to express my gratitude to everyone who gave me constructive criticism and helped me to fail-up from three decades of distorted realities. Special thanks to all those who gave me different perspectives, including Fox News, PBS, Real Vision, FT, HBR, Bloomberg, Ray Dalio, Hernando de Soto, Chamath Palihapitiya, Charlie Rose, GIFT (www.global-inst.com)...

This is a living manuscript and will continuously evolve based on your constructive feedback (contact @ www.EPM-Mavericks.com or www.Tiger-Rider.com)

Proceeds from this book will be donated to Mother Teresa Mission (Missionaries of Charity) or similar missions.

www.ingramcontent.com/pod-product-compliance
Lightning Source LLC
Chambersburg PA
CBHW040824300326
41914CB00070B/1656/J
9781956687095